Praise for *The Real Rules of Life*

"In this elegant, groundbreaking book, Ken shows us how to rise out of the ashes, turn adversity into opportunity, and transform our pain into love."
— **Jack Canfield,** co-author of the Chicken Soup for the Soul series

"When life kicks you below the belt—and sooner or later it's bound to—read this book. This must-have guide belongs in every library."
— **Ken Blanchard,** co-author of *The One Minute Manager*®
and *Great Leaders Grow*

*"For anyone who has ever had their heart broken, **The Real Rules of Life** provides powerful tools for healing and support. I highly recommend it."*
— **John Gray,** author of *Men Are from Mars, Women Are from Venus*

"I highly recommend this fine new book by Ken Druck. Read it and put his hard-won wisdom to work for you."
— **Gay Hendricks, Ph.D.,** author of *Five Wishes* and co-author of
The First Rule of Ten

"An amazing book whose time has come! It's real, it's accurate, and it offers insights each one of us can use. Read it, live it, and share it with everyone you know."
— **John Assaraf,** *New York Times* best-selling author of *The Answer* and
Having It All and CEO of PraxisNow.com

The
REAL RULES
of
LIFE

Also by Ken Druck, Ph.D.

The Secrets Men Keep: Breaking the Silence Barrier

Healing Your Life After the Loss of a Loved One

How to Talk to Your Kids About School Violence

The
REAL RULES
of
LIFE

Balancing Life's Terms
with Your Own

KEN DRUCK, PH.D.

HAY HOUSE, INC.
Carlsbad, California • New York City
London • Sydney • Johannesburg
Vancouver • Hong Kong • New Delhi

Published and distributed in the United States by: Hay House, Inc.: www.hayhouse.com® • *Published and distributed in Australia by:* Hay House Australia Pty. Ltd.: www.hayhouse.com.au • *Published and distributed in the United Kingdom by:* Hay House UK, Ltd.: www.hayhouse.co.uk • *Published and distributed in the Republic of South Africa by:* Hay House SA (Pty), Ltd.: www.hayhouse.co.za • *Distributed in Canada by:* Raincoast: www.raincoast.com • *Published in India by:* Hay House Publishers India: www.hayhouse.co.in

Cover design: Jonathan Friedman • *Interior design:* Jenny Richards

Library of Congress Cataloging-in-Publication Data

Druck, Ken.
  The real rules of life : balancing life's terms with your own / Ken Druck.
    p. cm.
  ISBN 978-1-4019-3971-7 (hbk. : alk. paper) 1. Conduct of life--Psychological aspects. I. Title.
  BF637.C5D78 2012
  158--dc23

                                                              2011050024

Hardcover ISBN: 978-1-4019-3971-7
Digital ISBN: 978-1-4019-3973-1

15 14 13 12 4 3 2 1
1st edition, May 2012

Printed in the United States of America

To Stefie, my "Earth daughter."
It is my honor . . . to be your father.
My love, forever.
Your PB

CONTENTS

ACKNOWLEDGMENTS

Writing a book may the closest a man gets to giving birth. Next to helping deliver my two daughters, Jenna and Stefie, writing this book is the most daunting act of creation I have undertaken in this lifetime.

And so, with all the feelings of a new father, I give my heartfelt thanks to my wise and beautiful daughters, dear friends and book reviewers, family, and beloved, Lisette, whose honesty, faith, and clarity guided and supported me through a long gestation, labor, and delivery.

Special thanks to Michael Levin for his steadfast editorial direction and guidance, and Reid Tracy and my new family at Hay House for embracing my newborn and helping me send it out into the world where it may flourish.

INTRODUCTION

L ife has rules.
They just may not be the ones you think.

It starts on the playground or sitting around the kitchen table as a kid. "The early bird gets the worm," we're told. "Slow and steady wins the race." "Play fair and people will play fair with you." "Good things happen to good people." "Keep your faith, and your dreams will come true."

From day one, these are the rules we're taught to live by. We get them from our parents, our teachers, and our culture at large, and as we grow older, they form the foundation of our hopes, expectations, and beliefs. In theory, it's a great system. All we have to do is treat people fairly, set positive goals, and work hard to achieve them. Since life is fair, everything works out in the end.

Here's the catch: these rules aren't real.

If you're reading this book, chances are you've already discovered that the rules you thought were real are not. Things you were told turned out not to be true. Life's not fair. Good things don't always happen to good people. Your heart breaks, you feel betrayed by people you trusted, and sometimes you even lose those you love. No matter how hard you work, how diligently you pray, or how respectfully you treat other people, the truth remains: life will have its say.

In this book, I want to share with you the Real Rules of Life. They're not the rules you've heard a hundred times before, and they're not always what you'd expect. Some of them are going to be a relief, a welcome "aha!" affirming what you have always known in your heart. Others may feel terribly uncomfortable and hit painfully close to home.

Together, they all make up the subtle, simple truths of how life really is. That includes life's many mysteries, blessings, uncertainties, and the vast unknowingness we're asked to live in day by day. At times, these truths can seem overwhelming. They can leave us feeling so empty that we just don't want to face them. Yet the chapters ahead will explain why it is in our best interest to do exactly that. Understanding and boldly coming to terms with how life really is, sooner rather than later, positions us to live the rest of our lives fully awake. Making peace with what we've been avoiding or running away from, perhaps since childhood, allows us to ripen as human beings.

We spend a lot of time and energy avoiding and denying the Real Rules of Life. We struggle within ourselves, trying desperately not to look these truths in the eyes. And yet, by acknowledging their existence, one by one, we can begin to make peace with life. Take the fact that we age, for example. Making peace with our own mortality, coming to terms with changes in our bodies as they slow and eventually break down, is one tough challenge. But doing this, as we will see, allows us to make the necessary adjustments to live more enjoyably and purposefully in the time we have. Apple founder and icon Steve Jobs, who died this past year, understood this. "Remembering that I will be dead soon," he said in a speech to Stanford graduates, "is the most important tool I've ever encountered to help me make the big choices in life. Because almost everything—all external expectations, all pride, all fear of embarrassment or failure—these things just fall away in the face of death, leaving only what is truly important."

We can also recognize that we will probably suffer heartbreaking losses and disappointments during the course of our lives. That we live in dangerous, risky, unsafe, and uncertain times, where so many things are out of our control. And, perhaps most important, that life's many blessings and gifts will pass us by unless we begin to count them.

So the question becomes: How do we deal with the reality of our lives? Courageously face our fears? And awaken? How do we not tie up all our energy in hiding, denying, repressing, pretending, avoiding, and hurrying through our days? How do we free ourselves so that we may embrace life's deep, rich joys and weather its sorrows? How do we become more humbly aware and accepting of how life really is—while living more boldly than ever? As if each day was a precious gift?

The Real Rules presented in this book will set you on the path of far greater awareness, more vibrant joy, and a deeper effectiveness in coping with life's ups and downs. It's not about doing it perfectly. It's about debunking the false rules and opening yourself up to the real ones. You'll discover that significantly greater clarity, personal effectiveness, peace, and contentment come when you understand life's terms—and how to balance them with your own.

We all travel different paths in this life. Some we choose. Some choose us. The path that chose me was one of loss. It was set into motion by one defining moment that transformed my life 15 years ago. The loss of my daughter, Jenna, and my life as her father, has brought me to where I am right now: writing about the lessons I've learned along life's long, uneven course.

Losing Jenna

In my 20s and 30s, I was fortunate to have what most would call a blessed life. My wife and I had two lovely daughters and a beautiful home near the ocean in San Diego, California. My private practice was thriving. And my creative juices were flowing. I was one of the first in my profession to use the concept of "executive coaching"—an approach that caught on like wildfire and grew into an industry. My clients included many leaders in business and government and a number of top-tier companies such as Microsoft, Pfizer, and IBM, all making their mark on the world.

By the 1980s, I'd established myself as a highly respected pioneer in the field of psychology and had written a landmark book called *The Secrets Men Keep*. I traveled the world, often with my family, giving workshops and lectures. I had the opportunity to appear multiple times on national programs such as *Oprah, Donahue,* and *Larry King Live*. Life was good. It seemed as though everything I'd been taught to believe was true—work hard, be a good husband and father, and your life will be blessed.

Then, on March 27, 1996, at 10 P.M., I received a phone call that changed my life forever. Four American students studying abroad with the Semester at Sea program had been killed in a bus accident in India. My 21-year-old daughter, Jenna, was one of them.

Jenna's death ended my life as I knew it. Up to that point, I'd been functioning under the assumption that I'd worked out a deal with life—if I was a good man and lived a good life, my daughters would somehow be protected. And suddenly I was seeing pictures of my daughter's body lying on a dirt road on the front page of *India Today*, had reporters from all over the world sitting vigil on my front lawn, greeted close friends and family arriving at our home hourly, and was learning the grim details of my daughter's death on CNN. In the spring of 1996, Real Rule #3 hit hard: There Are No Deals. We don't get to make deals with life.

Over the last 15 years, I've been coming to terms with the reality that we don't get to play God. None of us! We are not in control of much that happens in our lives. Our dreams don't always come true. In fact, sometimes the dreams we cherish the most evaporate before our very eyes.

I had so many dreams for Jenna's life. And Jenna had already begun fulfilling so many of her own. My daughter was on a trajectory for greatness—she was selected San Diego's "Young Woman Entrepreneur" at the age of 9. By 14 she was speaking publicly before adult audiences, and in high school she co-founded a leadership camp. She was chosen as a President's Leadership Institute Scholar and elected president of her sorority at the University of Colorado. She was also working part-time for MTV, managing the stage at Radio City Music Hall where the music video awards were held. Jenna was living her dreams and had big plans for the future. She had even met a "special boy." And then it all came to a senseless end.

How could this have happened? How?

I spent several years in utter devastation. The emotions I waded through were intense and all-consuming—grief, rage, betrayal, guilt, emptiness. There were times I just wanted to die. One moment, I had two beautiful daughters thriving in the world, a big home with dogs running in and out, and a family intact. The next moment, it had all turned to dust. Our three dogs became ill and, one by one, died. My wife of 25 years and I were no longer together. Jenna was gone, and my youngest daughter, Stefie, had moved out to start her own life. I was alone and broken, engulfed by what the ancients used to call "the dark night of the soul."

And then, slowly, bit by bit, I began climbing out of the bottomless pit called despair. I'd always heard that you have to take life one day at a time. At the beginning, a day was too much for me. An hour was even too long. One breath at a time was what I could handle. And so, breath by breath, with the love of family and friends, the support of my men's group (ten absolutely amazing guys who are all leaders in their own right), and the inspiration from bereaved fathers like the artist Monet, the composer Mahler, Abraham Lincoln, and Otto Frank (Anne's Dad), I began this long journey into a new and painfully unfamiliar life. A life without Jenna.

Each morning that first year, I went for a long walk by the ocean near my home and had a conversation with Jenna. I began referring to her as my "angel" daughter. One of the first things she "said" to me was, "Dad, this is not about you." It took me a long time to realize that she was right. At the time it seemed like it was all about me and my pain. But when I finally began to untangle myself from the web of sorrow and tragedy I was mired in, I came to accept that it's not about us, no matter how special (or entitled) we think we are. The Real Rules go beyond our personal experience and encompass something much bigger than ourselves. From the "conversations" I would have with my "angel daughter," Jenna, every day, I started referring to it as "the enormity." Learning to embrace the enormity beyond my own life helped me overcome the deepest despair. And in its place, I began to discover an even deeper wellspring of love and compassion.

As I began to look beyond my own grief, I found ways to reach out instead of cave in. I created a nonprofit foundation, the Jenna Druck Center, from the ashes of my loss. This included ministering to other families whose lives had been turned inside out by the loss of their children, as well as implementing a leadership program for girls—a program Jenna herself and her best friend, Pilar, had first envisioned as sophomores in high school.

My platform as a teacher–healer expanded, too. I was called upon to help out in several national tragedies, including the school shooting at Columbine, New York after 9/11, and Hurricane Katrina. My work became well recognized and I was honored with awards including "Distinguished Contribution to Psychology," "Visionary Leadership," and "Family Advocate of the Year." I was even invited to speak at prestigious universities such as The Harvard School of Public Health, professional conferences, synagogues, churches, and organizations such as YPO (The Young Presidents' Organization). And I became a regular guest on many local and national television shows like *Anderson Cooper 360*.

Moments of Truth

Each of us has moments in our life that demand every ounce of courage and strength we have, and then some. Not to mention our full attention. All of the superficial noise and static of the world fades away and we are touched at the very core of our being. For me, that moment was losing my daughter. But the path is not always loss. We can be equally shaken, and awakened, by a period of great adversity such as after a life-threatening illness, divorce, or retirement. We can also experience our moment of truth after something wonderful—the birth of a child, successful heart transplant, lifetime achievement award—or something wonderfully subtle, like the sun setting over the ocean, a butterfly landing on your shoulder, or a grandchild falling asleep in your arms. In these moments, we're invited to behold "the enormity" or totality of life. We become the clear observer of an unfiltered experience, and our soul is moved to a deep abiding awareness of how things really are—the suffering and the joy.

Whether your path is one of tragic loss, triumphant joy, or anything in between, it is my hope that rethinking the rules by which you've been living—and the ones I'm calling the "Real Rules"—will inspire a moment of truth for you. Show you how to make your life more of what you have always wanted it to be. And reveal not only the big picture of life, but the secrets that are hidden in the fine print.

The Fine Print of Life

Most of us glide through life under the tacit assumption that everything's going to be just fine. And we work hard to make it so. Inevitably, something (life) happens that changes everything. Our plans are derailed. Standing in the ashes of our plans, heartsick and face to face with risks, doubts, dangers, and possibilities that lurk in "the fine print," we ask, "How could this have happened?"

We close our eyes to the fine print of life most of the time. Who wants to read the "side effects" label of the chemotherapy drugs that may potentially save their life? Or hear that their beautiful 21-year-old daughter may die in a study abroad program? But when we truly understand life's terms, we see that it is filled with suffering and joy, ups and downs, clarity and confusion, good and bad. No matter what we do, we will never be immune to life's changes and losses: business failures, accidents and illnesses, divorce, and—at the darkest depths—the loss of a loved one. Sure as there will be joy, there will be heartache, confusion, conflict, and grief.

The fine print isn't there to just warn us of side effects, disclaimers, risks, and dangers. It awakens us to life's miracles, surprises, and startling revelations. The kind that brighten and transform our lives in one defining moment. The Real Rules you're about to consider can be very subtle and quietly hidden in the fine print of life.

Now, I'm not suggesting that we're always at the mercy of forces greater than ourselves, or should give up on boldly setting the terms by which we aspire to live. There's no excuse for not passionately pursuing our dreams and striving to become the highest and best expression of ourselves. This is our time and we need to make the most of it. Our challenge is to both go after what we want passionately and accept that, regardless of the plans we make, life will have its say. Getting through the tough times—and transforming adversity into opportunity—requires courage, humility, and getting real about the way things are.

Getting Real

Honesty, or getting real, is a theme that runs through every chapter of this book (and all of my coaching, consulting, and speaking) because it's a wise strategy for living (i.e., developing character, being a person of virtue, living with integrity and succeeding in relationships). It's also critical for dealing with all forms of adversity. Clichés like "When the going gets tough, the tough get going," are cute but don't tell us how to make changes in our lives. We all love a good locker room speech, and sometimes we need to be inspired to dig in and summon the courage to prevail. But we must also learn to get real and get serious about what it takes to effect change, starting with our own thinking and behavior. Cultivating and sharpening our most important and underutilized tool, our awareness, sets the stage for sustainable growth and change.

When it comes to dealing with real life, we need guideposts, or rules. We need to understand and come to terms with the Real Rules if we're going to attain the highest and best in ourselves, our relationships, and our life's work. Even if that starts with digging ourselves out of a hole. Clearing the air of confusion. Breaking free of demons and self-defeating patterns that hold us back. My journey over the last 15 years, fighting my way back into life after Jenna's death, has taken me deep into the fine print and helped me uncover The Real Rules of Life.

These rules gave me the awareness, perspective, and emotional freedom to navigate where I was and where I wanted to go. I think of them as kind of a GPS, helping me map out where I am on the road when I'm uncertain. Saving me time and aggravation. Just punch in the coordinates, and the invisible woman with the British accent will guide me there.

Of course, as we all know, reaching our desired destination isn't that simple. There are times when we get lost, confused, and completely turned around. That's when the "recalculating" feature of GPS comes in handy. Sometimes we have to push the RESET button in our minds, relax our defenses, and recalibrate ourselves. Or go online to update the software on our personal GPS so all the new roads are listed. This requires patience, flexibility, and calm determination, critical factors in making the necessary adjustments to change our trajectory and move our lives forward.

I urge you to apply these rules with patience and kindness. Reading a book like this, it's easy for our heads to fill up with self-criticism and self-doubt. We tell ourselves, "I'm not doing it right!" or "I've screwed it all up," or "I should have known/been doing this all along." Instead of harsh self-criticism, read *The Real Rules of Life* with kindness and self-compassion. Even the slightest increase in self-compassion will create more spaciousness in your heart and mind, more freedom to be human (and real), and more energy to get your personal house in order.

Let the rules speak to you. There is no wrong way to read this book, no wrong way to interpret these rules and apply them to your life. Maybe you'll resonate with three or four of these rules and focus on them. Perhaps one Real Rule in particular will speak to you. Also, since the Rules are arranged in no particular order, feel free to flip open to any rule and start reading, and to skip around.

The structure of *The Real Rules of Life* is simple: every chapter is dedicated to one of the Real Rules. Each rule represents one of the core realities I've learned in my awakening from grief the past 15 years and my experience as a confidant to literally thousands of people—all of whom I also consider to be *my* teachers.

Throughout this book you'll see Getting Real boxes, highlighting key ideas for each Real Rule. These are meant to distill what we're discussing into easily digestible nuggets. At the end of every chapter, there's a Real Action box. Think of these as takeaways, actionable steps that help you reflect on that particular Real Rule, explore the possibilities for making positive changes, and clear the path for that to happen. There are also a few suggested exercises embedded in the chapters themselves.

Treat this book as a workbook. Don't just passively turn the pages; write on them, dog-ear them, or cover them in sticky notes. Jot down action items (with timelines to hold yourself accountable) and do the suggested exercises that will benefit you with greater awareness. You may wish to keep a separate journal or share your "aha's" and the changes you're inspired to make with a trusted confidant, such as a friend or life coach. Ask for their personal feedback. Or go online to www.kendruck.com to see what other readers have to say about a particular Real Rule and to share your experiences interactively.

This book will help you pull back the veil and see the rules that truly govern your life and the lives of those around you. No fairy tales. No psychobabble. No spin. *The Real Rules of Life* is meant to empower you to be more honest with yourself and authentic in the way you are living. To inspire you to take off the blinders and go for it. And to guide you through actually making the changes you desire.

Understanding how life really is, coming to terms with and overcoming adversity, living in the light of life's true blessings, and embracing the enormity—this is the path now before you. Are you ready to begin the journey?

Real Rule #1

LIFE IS NOT FAIR:
It's More Than Fair

For most of my life, I lived under the assumption that life was essentially fair. The majority of us operate under this same principle, whether we know it or not. If we work hard to attain our dreams, we assume we'll be able to achieve them. If we have children, we assume they will grow up into upstanding adults. If we put our hearts and souls into our work, we assume we're going to get ahead. If we buy a house, we assume we're going to pay off our mortgage in 30 years.

Then, something happens. A husband betrays us. We're fired from our dream job. Our wife walks out the door and doesn't come back. A child gets strung out on drugs. A dear friend becomes ill. At some point, we all come face to face with the stark and naked truth: life isn't fair at all.

Up until my daughter Jenna's death, I was living under the false assumption that my daughters would always be protected; that nothing bad could happen to them. I felt magically entitled to a long and happy life for Jenna and Stefie. And for myself. It was as if by doing all the right things—having a nice home, living in an affluent community, striving to be a good parent—I had struck a deal with life. And life, being essentially fair, would honor that deal.

But, as I learned that night in 1996, life isn't fair. It's never been fair, and it never will be.

Things Happen. Or Do They?

We've all heard the sayings, "Things happen." And "Things happen for a reason." After Jenna died, I heard them a lot. In their attempt to make sense of her death, people attributed it to everything from bad luck to God's will. Someone even told me, "Everything works out for the best. God must have needed her in heaven."

Then there were the folks who attributed her death to karma. "It's all a part of the master plan," they explained. "Jenna was meant to die. It was her destiny."

The truth of my daughter's sudden, violent death, like many things, is unknowable, and it would have resonated with me if someone had just said so. It's our choice to believe what we wish and render our best guesses about why bad things happen, but every explanation of why this happened was completely unhelpful and unsatisfying to me.

We don't get to know with any certainty whether life is random. There are some wonderful arguments for a higher intelligence. A plan. An order. A direction this is all going. And there are some equally wonderful arguments to the contrary. What I'm saying is: it's beyond our capacity to know for sure what precise factors determine how things unfold in our lives. And why we die when we do. Or if there is even anything to be made sense of in matters like these.

However, that awareness should never stop us from feeling our way in the dark, from contemplating and/or investigating the "whys" of life. It's only natural that we want to know—to intuitively, spiritually, and even scientifically understand more and more about the secrets of the universe. Surely, a deeper, richer understanding of life and death could be helpful to any one of us in the long run, even if it shakes up our world at first.

Of course, there are certain questions that all the scientific research in the world is unlikely to explain. For example: what happens to us when we die?

Part of the mystery of death was revealed to me, as it often is, during

2

the time I spent with my daughter's "remains." Getting Jenna's body home from India was an arduous, difficult process, in the end only made possible by the help of President and Mrs. Clinton and their staff. Her body arrived from India the day before her funeral, and I went to be with her one last time before the burial.

Nothing I have ever experienced comes close to the unspeakable pain of holding my daughter's lifeless body in my arms. I needed to kiss and talk to her, to brush her hair from her eyes. I found myself searching for signs of life. But Jenna was no longer in her body. I had the distinct feeling that her spirit had moved on, and as I held her in my arms, I knew it.

When your child dies, all the theories you once had about life—the "Things happen" vs. "There's a higher power" debate—go from being an elective credit to the curriculum. You need to know where your child is! It's not very different than the questions you used to ask as a concerned parent—"Where are the kids tonight? What time are they going to be home?" When your child dies, you don't stop asking, "Where is my child?" Or scanning the universe for "signs" of their whereabouts.

Sometimes, on birthdays or holidays, I go to the cemetery where Jenna is buried. And I can hear her telling me, "Dad, what are you doing here? That grave with my name and picture on it? That's not me. You want to be with me? Then be with me. But I'm not here."

It's easy to get lost in theories about life and death. And humbled in our search for truth. We've all wondered: Is life a string of random events? Or is there a just and loving God overseeing all of this? Are we human beings having a spiritual experience, or spiritual beings having a human experience?

I don't have the answer to these questions. All I can say is, I don't know with any real certainty what death is. I can only bet my faith. Anyone who says they know for certain may be missing out on one of life's most fundamental and divine elements—its sense of mystery. Death can be an ugly and horrifying mystery, but the end of life can also be beautifully mystical and profound.

Getting Real—"The Duality of Life's Mystery"

The unbearable pain of loss and heartbreak can often make us ask, "Why?"

Yet we can also ask "Why?" for the blessings and gifts in our lives.

The truth is that it's all mystery. We have no way of knowing why sometimes our hearts are torn asunder, and other times, they're filled to overflowing.

Love is also one of life's great mysteries—and miracles. Whether it's romantic love, love between friends, or the love a parent has for a deceased child, loving and being loved is truly one of the most uplifting and confounding parts of being alive. But every yin has its yang, and the flipside of love is loss.

Losing a loved one means we must fight through the despair, the disillusionment, and all the beliefs we once held about "happily ever after" and "forever." We're going to feel heartsick, disoriented, and deeply sorrowful. It's written in the small print of life that, at some point in our lives, we will all be devastated by a loss. And that we, too, will die.

If we know this—that life isn't fair and losses are going to be a part of it—how do we equip ourselves and our children with a working knowledge of the Real Rules instead of placating them with sugar-coated myths, fairy tales, and quick fixes? How do we help our kids struggle with these issues and develop the kind of coping abilities they will need? And set a good example as their parents?

It's natural for every parent to want to protect his or her kids from the harsh realities, but if we overprotect them, they may never develop the ability to cope. On the other hand, carelessly putting them in overwhelming situations is foolhardy and even dangerous. How can we truly be there for our children in their times of loss, helping them cope with adversity rather than telling them to pick themselves up by their bootstraps, suck it up, and get over it?

Suck it Up, Grandpa

Years ago, I was giving a speech at a conference in Iowa when a middle-aged farmer told me a story I have never forgotten. This man had raised his son to be a real man's man. In his day it was all about being tough and strong; showing emotion was something that only sissies did. Even in times of great loss or pain, his mantra was, "Suck it up and move on." The man's son now had a son of his own, and had raised him in much the same way.

One day, the man was out plowing a field with his seven-year-old grandson when his tractor broke down. As he was trying to fix a blade, it fell and cut open his hand. He soon realized he was a mile from the house, bleeding to death, and couldn't move. Looking to his grandson, he said, "You have to get help for Grandpa. Please go to the house and get Grandma."

The little boy turned to his grandfather, saw the blood pouring out onto the ground, paused for a moment, and then said, "Grandpa, just suck it up!"

Wondering whether his grandson could grasp the urgency of the situation, he thought to himself, *What have I done?* The mantra he had preached his whole life—"Be a man!"—could very well have killed him.

Luckily, the boy did run for help, and the man's life was saved. But the parable is evident: just telling our kids to "suck it up" or "fight back" in times of pain or loss is not always the answer. What we teach our children can mean the difference between life and death.

Finding Strength in Humility

We all experience moments of humility. They may come at our quietest moments late at night, as we fall across the finish line after running 26.2 miles, or after the loss of a job, career, 401(k), spouse, or dear friend. Whatever the case may be, these defining moments reveal our core values. Character. And our faith. Sometimes we want to be anything but humble; we'd rather be seething mad. "I've done everything that's been asked of me!" we cry out. "I do every damn thing right. What the hell did I ever do to deserve this?"

In moments like this, "suck it up" or "the glass is half full" just isn't going to cut it. So if that's not the answer, then what is? How do we cope with life's setbacks? How do we come to terms with the fact that sometimes, life is going to hurt like hell?

The answer is: with great humility. There are times of adversity in life when surrender and humility are the most helpful things we can experience. Life brings all of us to our knees. We're at the mercy of a reality that is so much bigger than our ability to comprehend it. We can all feel so small, so insignificant, and so powerless.

Showing humility goes so much farther than trying to "suck it up" or invoke some other rough-and-ready cliché. In fact, we can flip through our book of clichés for sayings that prop us up and provide temporary relief, but in reality, we're just flipping through blank pages. Those clichés may work some of the time. And may last just long enough to get us through the night. But at some point, they're going to be useless if not harmful. And it is in those moments that humility can get us through.

Being brought to your knees is different than lying down and taking it. In fact I'd advise you, once again, not to dismiss the feelings of disappointment and despair that may arise. Take a moment to really feel the unfairness and outrage of what has happened. Acknowledging these feelings and moving toward a place of true optimism may mean that you *allow* yourself to feel defeated. Don't self-medicate with trite clichés, busyness, or a few drinks. On the contrary: give yourself some time to feel sad, helpless, angry, overwhelmed or scared since that is how you really feel. You didn't sign up for this. But here it is. So just let yourself feel genuinely angry and disappointed.

Getting Real—"Real Humility"

Surrendering doesn't mean giving up or copping out. It's about allowing all the feelings to simply be, without judging them or yourself.

And go from there.

Let's say you just got fired from your job. Say, "Damn!" In fact, be generous with yourself. Give yourself ten "Damn-its!" Voice your objection! Give yourself a chance to say, "This really sucks." And let yourself feel it. Once you've gotten it all out, take a deep breath. Feel the relief that comes from clearing frustration and anger that have been building up. Make space for new feelings. You never know, after all, what's around the corner. You may get the best job you've ever had as a result of quitting the old one. You just don't know. Is this way of thinking "negative"? Is it unproductive whining and complaining? Far from it: I'm a very positive person. What I'm "anti" is when people are encouraged to sweep their true feelings under the rug. Sometimes this happens in the "positive thinking" community, but it's just as likely to happen outside of it. And after all the grief work I've done with people whose worlds have been turned upside down, I truly believe that it's counterproductive for people to be talked out of what they're feeling by positive thinking or to undergo a "spiritual bypass." We can't just skip over what we're experiencing because "It's a part of God's plan," "It's destiny," or, "God will handle it." Frankly, that "should feel" approach just doesn't work when it comes to coping with real life. Better to get real.

Getting Real—"Attentive Patience"

Humility is attentive patience. — Simone Weil

My own healing process took being able to be very angry, and to really feel that anger. I remember railing and raging against God for several hours straight. I wanted to spit in the face of the universe for allowing my daughter to die. I had to get that anger out to arrive at a place where I could actually imagine a tear in the eye of God. God was crying with me over my loss. I no longer felt separate and alone or blamed God.

That experience changed everything. Had I not had the safety and permission to get angry at God, or if I had tried to stuff it, hide it, deny

7

it, repress it, hurry it, and avoid it, I never could have moved to a place of deeper understanding about God and how life really is.

I'm not saying you need to rage and rail at God. To each his own—we all respond differently to loss. And to adversity. What I'm saying is that you have to allow yourself to have whatever experience you're having. To be real! It is the processing of these emotions that deepen us, strengthen our heart, and teach us to cope with "real" life. And eventually give us the ability to crawl out of the ashes of adversity. And if someone—anyone—tries to take that away and put a feel-good "positive spin" on the situation, to fix or rescue us from ourselves, then they've circumvented a process of deepening, growth, coming to terms, and healing.

Helping people feel safe and respected in the presence of a great sorrow is truly sacred. When I work alongside individuals and families who have experienced the loss of a family member, my goal is to be with them. To really be with them, encouraging them to share whatever it is they might be feeling. Knowing it's okay to feel totally shattered and defenseless against their own sorrow in that moment allows the next moment to be different. They discover they are not alone, not going crazy, and will, in time, garner the strength to go on.

An Ongoing Paradox

There's no denying it: life isn't fair. But, paradoxically, if you really think about it, life is more than fair. It's even a miracle that we can sustain life as we do. It is also in our moments of greatest loss and brokenness that we are in a position to feel a greater sense of hope, faith, and wholeness.

It is in our unknowingness, staring into the abyss, that we often uncover life's most profound truths. Gratitude. Perspective. Faith. It is in these unfiltered, transformational moments that we can access an understanding and reverence for what life really is. A moment of utter emptiness turns into one of fullness. Silence becomes pregnant with meaning. Doubt yields to deeper understanding. The connections to the people in our lives become precious. We find an unfamiliar comfort in stillness. We discover humor and lightheartedness in irreverence. We see that we are part of the mystery of life, and surrendering to this knowledge helps us rise out of our despair.

Getting Real—"From the Ashes"

Life isn't fair . . . but it's more than fair at the same time.

Sometimes genuine hopefulness comes from the hardest moments in our lives—a phoenix rising from the ashes of our loss. As 13th-century poet Rumi wrote, "Grief can be the garden of compassion."

We live in a society that prescribes a pill for every pain. A diversion for every emptiness. A fix for every problem. There is so little room for people to sit in a moment of uncertainty, to face the emptiness that follows a loss. But if we can sit in that moment, if we can just stay with it long enough, we find the fullness behind the emptiness. The blessing behind the pain. The certainty behind the doubt. Sometimes it's as simple as relinquishing control and allowing ourselves to breathe.

I'm not talking about manufactured, synthetic hope or faith. I'm talking about true hopefulness, the kind that arises out of humility. These are the things that deepen us and build our character, making us into stronger, better, more resilient versions of ourselves. These are also the things that turn us into invaluable resources for other people, because we become safe, wise, and judgment-free—clear and unbiased witnesses to stand beside others whose dreams have been shattered. And hold a place of hope for them.

As our understanding that life isn't fair grows deeper, it ironically gives us a significantly greater capacity to recognize all the ways that life is more than fair. To appreciate those ways. To savor them. To live in gratitude.

My morning hikes into the canyons of Torrey Pines State Beach that I alluded to before often take the form of a walking meditation. As I trudge up the hill to the top, I'm thinking about all the ways life has been unfair. How much of a struggle things are. In my head is nothing but static and noise. I allow myself to vent about all the frustration and anger and unfairness of life, things that make life feel like an uphill battle and which are standing in the way of my making it to the top. I might even talk aloud to myself about it or let out a few choice words directed at someone with whom I am upset. It's taken me a while to learn how to let these upsets flow through me without judgment.

As I reach the top of the hill, and begin walking down the trail to the beach, the path is winding and uneven. I have to pay attention to each step. I practice staying in the moment as I make my way down the hill through the canyons. I am captivated by the beauty of the light rising on the trees, the smell of rosemary and sage, the sight of the ocean where pelicans and dolphins await.

Just before I reach the ocean, I stop at my special perch, take a deep breath, and behold the beautiful, awe-inspiring ocean with an entire world beneath its surface. By the time I get down to the beach, my mood is one of gratitude. I think about every single thing, even the tiniest, most microscopic thing that I have to be grateful for; the love of my earth and angel daughters, my family and dear friends; for the ability to do the work I do, my health, the kindnesses people have shown me, all that is good and right in the world, the majesty of nature, to be able to walk on this beautiful beach and, of course, for my life.

Giving thanks for things great and small, I am sometimes brought to tears. There is such beauty and abundance, at any given moment, all around us . . . if we simply open ourselves up to it.

As I make my way home from the beach, I'm often struck by the reality that I can't just open myself to one side; life is a package deal. Only when I open myself to life's cruel and brutal unfairness and its miraculous fairness can I begin to make peace with life as it really is.

✧ ✧ ✧

Real Action

RR#1 TAKEAWAYS

EXERCISE #1 To sharpen your self-awareness, ask, "Do I expect life to be fair? Am I holding a grudge against life—for hurting me or letting me down?"

EXERCISE # 2 If you are, list the ways life has let you down. Next to each one write "What would have to happen for me to let go of my grudge is_____."

Consider talking about this exercise with a trusted friend or advisor.

EXERCISE #3 Place a check next to those actions that would help you adopt more of an attitude of humility in life's most unfair moments:

❏ Start each day by taking a moment to reflect on the gifts and blessings, hardships and setbacks, in my life.

❏ Remember to breathe and allow the feelings to wash over me like water when I'm upset and have suffered a setback. Let them come without judgment . . . and then, let them go.

❏ Allow the seeds of hope to take root in even the most unexpected of places—like a tender green plant sprouting from under a boulder.

❏ Use what I have learned to support a friend who is currently facing a hardship, since our personal losses forge us into stronger, more empathetic supporters for our family and friends.

Real Rule #2

AROUND EVERY CORNER:
Keeping an Open Heart

Years ago, a woman in her mid-20s named Julie came to one of my Executive Couple workshops. Julie had spent most of her 20s entangled in one bad relationship after another; all the men in her life turned out to be emotionally unavailable or, worse, emotionally abusive. She called them her "bad boys." After struggling through a series of painful breakups, she adopted the all-too-common mantra: "There just aren't any good men out there." Julie confessed that living by this mantra was making her feel even more hopeless. She wanted to feel hopeful again but realized it would have to happen in a whole new way. She would have to change.

At the workshop, which she attended alone, Julie really opened up to Real Rule #2: Around Every Corner. Simply put, it means "Don't give up!" Whether you've been blessed with good fortune or had nothing but bad luck, there is always the possibility that the thing you want the most—whether it's the perfect job, the love of your life, a medical miracle to save your sister's life, or to break free of an old relationship pattern—may be waiting just around the corner.

"Break out of your old pattern of choosing bad boys," I told Julie as the workshop concluded, "and see what happens. You never know."

Nearly a decade later, I heard from Julie again. Sure enough, in her 30s, she got into counseling and worked hard to break her pattern. And sure enough, her "luck" had changed. She met a nice man who was smart, funny, and kind. She called him her "good boy." After dating for two years, they were married. Both were happy and eager to begin a family—something Julie had always dreamed about.

But, as the months turned into years, it had become clear that Julie and her husband were unable to get pregnant. After more than six years of trying to have a baby, the pressure and disappointment had taken their toll. Julie was 38 years old, and feeling very disheartened. For the second time in her life, Julie had all but given up hope. But this time she had Real Rule #2 to fall back on and she persisted in getting professional help from a wonderful fertility doctor.

I recently received an e-mail from Julie. Attached to the e-mail was a picture of Julie and her husband holding their newborn baby girl.

Our hearts and minds often shut down after a loss or setback. This is natural. We defend ourselves against any further hurt by retreating. We harden and/or numb our hearts. Yet, staying open is often the best protection, and our best insurance that things will turn around. It's completely understandable that we take time off to heal, but hiding behind a protective wall is not a good long-term strategy.

We all have infinite possibilities waiting for us around every corner. It could be something as simple as a surprise visit from an old friend, an unexpected gift in the mail, or a new business opportunity. Or it could be as profound as the birth of a child or a kidney transplant that gives new life to a beloved grandfather. It's the person who loses the love of their life and then, when they least expect it, meets someone wonderful and is given another chance at love.

There may be times you stop believing in yourself or feel defeated and want to give up. All you have is a faint hope. At these times, my buddy Asa, a former Marine, used to say, "We just keep on keeping on." This means keeping an open heart and mind, waiting for the rainbow that appears after a hard rain. The kindness and generosity that appear after a tragedy. The laughter that arises from despair. Learning to effectively manage disappointment and keep hope alive is something we can all spend the rest of our lives mastering. It takes great courage and faith.

When to Let Go and When to Push Forward

Each of us holds a world of hope and possibility in our hearts. Though the details may differ, at the core we all want the same things— lives rich with love, health, and meaning for ourselves and those we love. Sometimes the revelation that will turn things around and ignite a whole new chapter in our life is just beyond our awareness, waiting for us to do one of two things: let go, or push in.

How many of us have experienced the freedom of relief that comes when we finally let go of something? Maybe it was a bad relationship you stayed in too long. Or a job that was holding you down—one you kept in the interest of security but was never your passion. Maybe it was a project that never seemed to ever get any traction. It could have been a certain approach to parenting one of your kids that just wasn't working, or a long-standing grudge with a family member. Letting go and moving on, even in the most stubborn situations, is something we'll deal with throughout this book. But let's start with one of the most powerful and underutilized tools for letting go: forgiveness.

To forgive, or ask for forgiveness with a sincere apology, makes space for change and even reconciliation. A simple apology can result in a huge shift in your life and relationships. It can lift a tremendous burden from your heart and free up energy in your life.

At the other end of the spectrum from letting go is pushing forward. When I say "push forward," I'm talking about moving boldly into something new—even if it's scary. It's human nature to create stable, safe, and secure environments for ourselves. Comfort zones. In the beginning, that kind of predictability creates security and structure for our lives, which is a good thing. But there comes a point of diminishing returns where we start losing freedom. We're just going through the motions, out of habit. Our elasticity and excitement begin to fade, and that's when we need to reinvent ourselves. It's time to push the REFRESH button.

It takes courage to push that button. It may mean confronting an old, familiar situation or even starting over. We're forced to ask ourselves, "What now? What do I want to change in myself or my situation?" If we're seeking an honest answer to those questions, we'll probably discover the need for making at least a few mid-course corrections. And sometimes, even turning the ship around, adjusting the sails, and heading in another direction.

Getting Real—"Letting Go" and "Pushing Forward"

Letting go means detaching ourselves from whatever is holding us back, whether it's a bad relationship, an unfulfilling job, or a destructive way of thinking. **Pushing forward** means taking a leap of faith as a way to embrace new opportunities. Both of these tactics open our hearts, minds, and lives to new possibilities.

Most of us don't like change. We're happier where it's safe and warm. Yet we have to acknowledge when it's time to draw the line and make a change. Even if it's as subtle as changing the ways we feel—like giving up the anger at somebody we've held at a distance for years, or needing to be right. It could be anyone from your former boss to your parents to your ex-wife; the point is, letting go of the anger that's been eating away at you could completely change the way you feel and help you move forward.

The change around the corner for you could be as simple as adding something "novel" to your life. It's signing up for the dance or singing class you've always wanted to take. Maybe you've said for years that you wanted to work with your hands, and there's a new class at the community center. Perhaps you finally have the opportunity to learn a new language, start your own company, or begin to take Fridays off. Sometimes these changes are the ones that help us redefine and set the stage for new and wonderful chapters of our lives.

For Julie, working hard to change a deep-seated pattern paid off through meeting the love of her life and having a child. For another client of mine, it was adding an hour of yoga and meditation to his daily schedule that opened up possibilities he never dreamed of, as he discovered within himself the ability to quiet his own thoughts. He literally felt like a new man. Ways of changing our lives and ourselves are as limitless as we make them. Discovering a whole new world of possibility may be closer and less complicated than you think.

I'm not saying you always need to look to make a shift in your life. Shifts often happen automatically. What you have to do is pay attention to what is already shifting in you. What has your system already begun working to change? Begin to notice the slightest shift inside of you by tuning in and really listening to yourself.

If you're the kind of person who tends to hold back and resists change, you might want to push in gently. If you're the kind of person who pushes in too hard and tries to force change, you might want to hold back a little bit. But the important thing is simply noticing your own shifting tides rolling in and out. The sands will continue to shift in your life; what matters is that you take the time to notice. And then take action. We'll take time to read the newspaper and watch the news every day but not a minute to reflect on "the news" from within.

The Sublime of the Subtle

How often do we miss the subtleties in our lives? As the saying goes, "The fish is the last to discover the ocean." We drive through our neighborhoods every day, for years on end. Then, the first day we go for a walk, we see the most beautiful tree in front of our neighbor's house. It's always been there—but we've never really seen it! Like many things, we've been too busy rushing and hurrying through our lives to ever really notice it before.

Getting Real—"Tuning In"

Tuning in means taking the time to check in with yourself. Whether it's a few minutes of relaxation when you wake up in the morning or incorporating a meditation practice into your daily routine, take time to notice and sit with where you are spiritually and emotionally.

Sometimes we get so caught up in the details of everyday life that we miss out on the subtle treasures. We miss them because we're oblivious to them. In fact we may even blow right past them every day! And yet, if we allow ourselves to notice and even behold these things for more than just a moment, something changes in us. We begin to notice the subtle yet profound truths about ourselves and the world around us. It's a kind of awakening. Maybe crucial insight is given to us in a quiet moment, or a dream. Or an upsetting moment we would ordinarily try to dismiss because we don't like being upset. Or a crisis that threatens our well-being and even our life. Or even the disturbing behavior of someone we love that can no longer be ignored.

Years ago, I had the opportunity to meet a wonderful man named James Harvey, the former CEO of Transamerica. While interviewing Jim for a book I was writing with his mentor, Dr. Meyer Friedman, pioneer of type-A behavior, we met in his office at the apex of the Transamerica Pyramid in downtown San Francisco. I've never seen an office with such a spectacular view. The city of San Francisco was literally at his feet.

Jim had just undergone quadruple bypass surgery after nearly losing his life to a heart attack. And as we sat there at the top of the San Francisco skyline, he began to point out the landmarks below. Jim took me on a tour of the entire city as we looked curiously out of his windows and onto the world like two boys. He showed me where an earthquake had hit, where the art center was, and the weather system coming in over Sausalito.

"Before my surgery," he confessed, "I never noticed any of this." After a brush with death, he was finally able to see the beauty that was all around him. Instead of pushing on from one task to the next, which was part of his driven, type-A lifestyle, he was taking time to stop and behold the world from his perch literally at the top of the world. But until his heart attack, he couldn't see it. He didn't appreciate what he had; he was totally oblivious to it. Ironically, it took his near-death experience to save and enhance his life.

Sometimes we need a crisis to experience a shift. When our health is threatened, it awakens something in us, and we embrace life like never before. Sometimes we need to get sick to get better.

Jim was able to slow down and open his eyes to the beauty all around him, even amid the fiercely competitive world of business.

We don't have to wait until we almost die, or get divorced, or lose our job, to begin to live. Whether we utilize it or not, we're all given psychological, spiritual, and physical "software" that has the capacity to help us notice and process these things. Unfortunately, we pick up on such a small percentage of what we're capable of noticing. We blow right past the more subtle moments and opportunities, intimacies and intricacies, whereas if we learn to slow down and pay closer attention, we can be so much more alive, aware, and effective.

Real Rule #2 is about discovering within ourselves, and in the world, the greater possibilities around every corner. It's about opening ourselves to moments of joy, beauty, and calm as we bear witness to life's miracles. It's about opening to the enormity. The decision to awaken to the subtle is very personal. It begins with slowing down and becoming more aware and is made real with action. We can block out time for gentle yoga. We can go make an apology to someone we care about, to make amends. We can take a new class or read a new book. We can empower ourselves, doing a million and one things—or nothing at all—to bring about that brighter, sunnier day. But first we have to open our eyes, clear our minds, and begin to read from the fine print of life.

Getting Unstuck

Almost all of us have a history of hitting brick walls at some time in our lives. We find ourselves feeling confined, stuck, and trapped. Helpless, with no way out. Defeated and on the verge of giving up. We feel like we've tested all the possibilities already, and none of them work. It's as though every time we try to escape, we hit that wall again. As a result, we've lost faith in ourselves, others, and life itself. *Sure, I know what's around that corner,* the defeated think. *Just another brick wall.*

Getting unstuck can be tricky business. And don't let anyone try to convince you it's not. It usually happens in small increments and subtle movements. You don't have to think radically; it doesn't always mean quitting your job, leaving your spouse and family, or going to India to live in an ashram. It's best to start small. With a deep breath. And a reaffirmation.

What would it look like if, step by step, you began to free yourself of the guilt, fear, anger, anxiety, and harsh self-criticism that imprison you? And to open to those greater possibilities, bit by bit? What might be the first step to getting rid of whatever is hurting you and holding you back? What would it take for you to begin to believe in yourself and to dream once again?

Here's the key: You've got to clear the air! Get it out and let it go! For many years, I've been using a "clearing exercise" my clients tell me is their favorite. Why? Because it clears the air of emotions like anger and frees them to actually move forward. Especially in their most intimate relationships. It's a natural energy boost.

The first step is to write down 25 things you're angry (even furious) about. Direct your comments at a specific individual or group. If it's yourself you're angry at, direct the comments toward you. Each sentence begins with the words, "Screw you for . . ." Your job is to complete the sentence, holding nothing back! Don't mince words (even if you've been taught it's not okay to talk this way). Let 'em have it! Give 'em hell for what they did, or didn't do. And don't let up until you reach 25. After you're done writing them out, read them aloud, like you are actually saying these things to the person. This is an essential step for "clearing." You may be surprised at just how much anger you've been carrying around all this time.

After you've finished *clearing* your anger (harmlessly acknowledging the emotions you've been carrying around inside), get ready for step 2 of this exercise. In this step, your job is to give thanks—instead of hell—to the same individual or group. If you're ready to go, get started, but if you need to take a break feel free to take whatever time you need.

Once you're ready, begin each sentence with "Thank you for . . ." and list 25 things you're grateful for. Whether they're big or little things, get everything you're grateful for out on the table (and don't be surprised if you shed a few tears in the process). Now read them aloud as if the person were really there. Expressing your gratitude can elicit very intense feelings, and long-forgotten memories that serve as helpful reminders. Telling someone what they really mean to you can be very freeing.

This exercise is designed to clear and open your heart. It may inspire you to actually sit down and clear your emotions with somebody. Or to tell someone how grateful you are. Your reason for clearing the past with someone should be considered carefully. As should your expectations—and your approach. Healing and reconciliation are good reasons. Retribution and punishment are not.

Expressing the depth of our emotions, from rage to gratitude, helps us reconcile the painful past, even if only in our own hearts and minds, and clear the path for an uncluttered future.

Clearing the air with ourselves, and getting unstuck, almost always begins with self-compassion and kindness. A gentle acceptance that we are all a work in progress and recognition that there is no benefit in beating ourselves up for the past, the present, or for an unsecured future. If there's to be a better life ahead, you must learn to be truly kind to yourself. To be encouraging and patient with yourself. To disarm the critic and silence the admonitions. To diffuse the guilt. To take a deep breath, clear the air of deeply held resentments, and change the tone of your voice to patient and encouraging. To let go of some part of the painful past every day, and slowly step into the warm light of your life—and its greater possibilities.

✦ ✦ ✦

Real Action

RR#2 TAKEAWAYS

EXERCISE #1 How do you rate yourself in the area of managing disappointment and hope on a scale from 1 to 10 (with 10 being "very effective")?

EXERCISE #2 When it comes to feelings, do you tend to hold on or let go, express, or repress them?

EXERCISE #3 Is there some part of your life where you feel stuck and need to break out? Name it.

EXERCISE #4 What patterns hold you down/back and keep you stuck? What could you do to free yourself?

EXERCISE #5 Here are some ways to open up time and space in your life to greater, richer possibilities. Place a check next to the ones you're willing to try:

❏ Sign up for a gentle yoga or meditation class.

❏ Take a slow walk in my neighborhood (if it's safe to do so) observing everything in sight.

❏ Forgive someone you've been holding a grudge against, or someone with whom you're angry. Ask to be forgiven and do something to demonstrate or "make up" for what you did or did not do.

❏ Find an activity you love—something simple and attainable, like cooking, gardening, or crossword puzzles. While you do this activity, cultivate a state of quiet awareness. Use your activity as a chance to "tune in."

Real Rule #3

THERE ARE NO DEALS:
Life's Real Terms

Our Secret Worlds

Each of us has a secret world that we inhabit. This world is filled with private conversations—with ourselves, with our angels, with our God. These conversations form the unspoken, unwritten, unconscious assumptions and agreements we think we have with the universe. No one wants to feel like they're at the mercy of a harsh and random world.

Sometimes our secret agreements never come to our level of consciousness. But when they do, it's typically because the cover has been ripped off, and suddenly our private conversations are exposed for what they are: hopeful attempts to feel like we have some semblance of control over our lives. Without notice, our illusion of safety and security is ruptured, and we feel hung out to dry. Disillusioned and despairing. Abandoned.

Human beings are deal-makers from the get go. Whether we're trying to get a salesman to knock a few bucks off the sticker price or we're defining the terms of a new relationship with our business partner, we always want to negotiate the best deal for ourselves. It's natural that we want to represent our best interest; after all, if we don't look out for our own interest, who will? And as good advocates on our own behalf, it only makes sense that we try to bargain with life when it gives us terms we don't like.

Getting Real—"The Full Disclosure Clause"

There's no way for us to really know ourselves or our life trajectory until we know the unspoken agreements we think we've made with the universe.

In order to live in the world authentically, we have to be willing to uncover all the deals. It's like going to an attorney for the first time. "Okay," the attorney asks. "In order to build your case, I need to know what other agreements, assumptions, and expectations you have. Tell me everything."

Except this time, instead of an attorney, you have to disclose those things to yourself (and sometimes to a therapist, spiritual advisor, or life coach). This is the first step to breaking free of these unwritten deals and beginning to come to terms with life as it really is. No fairy tales, made-up stories, or illusions.

Once you've identified them, you can acknowledge that these are the assumptions on which you've been basing most of your life. And you can begin to gradually let them go, because in real life, there are no deals.

Each of us has thought we had a deal—only to have it fall apart before our very eyes. Whether we invested our life savings in a Ponzi scheme, our hopes in a man or woman, or our future in a home, we've all suffered humiliation and sorrow when things didn't go as planned.

Detours, delays, betrayals, and other unexpected changes happen in everyday life as well. They throw us off course, create tremendous stress, and force us to revert to, or create, a Plan B. For example, we leave 15 minutes early for our child's first school recital—only to be caught in traffic and show up half an hour late. We plan a romantic evening with our beloved only to be handed three hours of work by our new boss just as we're leaving the office. Our flight is delayed by a snowstorm 2,000 miles away, causing us to miss our high-school reunion. Our team is up by three runs in the ninth inning of the deciding game of the National League playoffs—only to lose their lead and the game. Disappointment, inconvenience, loss, and change are simply a part of life.

What if we begin to live with the idea that there are no deals? No magic bullets? No bargaining? No immunity? No complete certainty? That life is what it is? That it's going to be what it's going to be—a mystery unfolding?

If we accept those truths, we get to live with the uncertainties and unknowns of life, including perhaps the most unpredictable thing of all, how long we're going to live. There's no negotiability with death; someday we're all going to die. But since we don't get a final say about when that's going to happen, how are we supposed to live? Why not let go of at least some of the fear and embrace the unknown and unknowable elements of death? Cherish every moment that we have? Hold our beliefs about what happens when we die as our "faith"?

With this approach to life, every day becomes sacred. Every relationship becomes a chance for a true connection and meeting between two people. What if we begin to really cherish the people in our lives and the privilege of being with them every day? And treat ourselves in the same way, championing our health and doing things that will give us a better chance at a longer, happier life?

We're not bad or crazy people for making secret deals with life. Most of us have a Plan A and even a Plan B—we're hedging our bets on all sides. That's perfectly normal. But what if you took all the energy you invest in bargaining with life and faced the idea that there are no deals; just life on life's terms? We can have a profound influence on our lives—prolong them, or bring grace, imagination, relevance, greater peace, and love to them—but ultimately, we don't get to play God.

How might you improve the quality of the time you have been given? Learn to move with greater ease when dealing with life's unexpecteds? Learn to live in the joy and delight of what you do have . . .

right now? The possibilities for making this shift were best articulated by John Lennon in his song, "Imagine." Lennon and his wife, Yoko Ono, opened millions of hearts and minds to new possibilities for individual and global peace. Their formula was to hold our unknowingness with grace and humility, instead of righteousness and fear.

The Real Deal

Our need for a deal is often rooted in our innermost fears and desires. Since we don't know what's going to happen and don't really have control, we choose beliefs and set a course that help us make sense of the world—and that makes life, and even death, appear predictable.

But here's the real deal: there's no real future in dwelling on the future.

The future is in this moment, not somewhere else. We can't spend our whole lives playing the "I'll be happy when . . ." game. Bending and shaping everything to fit our beliefs. Postponing everything from happiness to forgiveness to good health to love. Justifying that the ends will be well worth the means it took to get there. Real joy is in the gift and the blessing of feeling comfortable in your own skin—right now. Heaven is here not there. Our greatest challenge and opportunity is in living in the gratitude and the grace of this fleeting, eternal moment. Life is not something that's going to happen. It's happening right here, right now! A life of integrity and meaning begins with being present and showing up in the moment of one's own life. Moment after moment.

A friend once told me, "My dog is happy with one bone. He didn't say, 'How many bones do I have in Chicago? How many bones do I have on Wall Street?'" If a dog can do it, so can you and I. It's time to unlock the joy and bounty of living life in the present tense (the irony, of course, is that the keys to a better future are often right here, right now, under our noses).

Getting Real—"The Bone Mentality"

Dogs like to keep it simple. And they're pretty happy creatures. If you can focus on what you have in the present, you'll be a lot happier, too.

The bad news is: there are no deals.

The good news is: you don't need a deal to find the deepest riches that this life has to offer. To find true significance and peace—focus on the now. The divinity is right here in this moment. It always has been. It's our job to open ourselves up to life, and to not blow past it in our frenzied search for the next bone. Allow this moment to be what it is, to be enough. Imperfect, flawed, full of uncertainty, and divine.

You're at the table with a great feast laid out before you. There are no deals . . . but there's so much more than that. At any given moment, you can partake in the vibrant fruits of awareness, of experience, of intelligence, of consciousness. And you, just like all around you, are a part of it. Our greatest challenge, as always, is to get out of our own way. To awaken. To have courage and faith.

◦ ◦ ◦

Real Action

RR#3 TAKEAWAYS

The unspoken deals we've made with life are often holding us back from really experiencing life at its best. Bring these assumptions to the surface and confront their validity. Consider and make peace with life's real terms.

EXERCISE #1 Write down your answers to the following questions:

- What are the "deals" you've made with life? For example, "I feel immune from anything bad happening to me because I eat right, pray, go to church, and work out regularly."

- In what ways might life's real terms conflict with the deals you've made?

- Finish this sentence, "If there are no deals, then I will _____."

- List five things you could do to practice living more in the present moment.

EXERCISE #2 Ask someone who really knows you what deals they think you've made with life.

Real Rule #4

RUNNING FROM REALITY TAKES ENERGY:
Truth as Courage

People talk a lot about the struggling economy. It's the buzzword on everybody's lips. I want to talk about the economy, too . . . the finite amount of energy that each of us has to stage our lives—and what we do with it.

Our energy can get caught up in all sorts of things. There are the classical examples—people who've spent three or five or seven years in law school or med school, and when they finally graduate, they realize the tremendous pressure they were under and how much it took out of them. Or people who spend decades in a go-nowhere marriage they cannot seem to either fix or end. But these are only the obvious examples. Each of us has a limited amount of time and energy. How we spend it is something only we really know. We may be running away from something or running toward something, but either way, our time and energy is being invested somewhere. And typically, we're so caught up in the daily matters of life that we lose touch with what it's costing us to live this way.

Think of it like carrying a 100-pound pack on your back. After a while, you get so used to it that you forget you're lugging 100 pounds of extra weight with you everywhere you go. You're not even sure about what's in that pack anymore. You've stopped feeling like you have a choice. So you continue to carry it around, doing what comes "naturally," bearing the weight of it. We all possess a remarkable ability to rationalize tying up all that energy as the price of doing business. One of the burdens we must bear.

Now imagine the following. What if you could just drop that 100-pound pack? What would happen if you could take it off your back, set it down on the floor, get up, and walk away? How would that feel?

What would happen if we stopped running long enough to take inventory of how we're allocating and investing our time and energy? If we unburdened and freed ourselves of all the hidden pressure, guilt, resentment, self-doubt, and hopelessness that we carry around? If suddenly we weren't carrying that pack around anymore, squandering our limited time and energy? What then? To start, we'd have freed up some energy to take honest inventory of what we have been doing, look at our options, and actually begin to do the things that bring greater meaning, relevance, and joy to our lives.

You've probably experienced this kind of "freeing" experience to some degree before. Perhaps on a vacation. On a rainy Sunday. Or during a heavy snowstorm when they had to cancel work. Maybe you waited for years for that big promotion, and when it finally came, you suddenly felt freed to do all the things you wanted to do. Or you finally got so angry and frustrated at someone that you broke your silence and spoke up. Instant relief flooded over you, offering you the strength and breathing room to finally have things the way *you'd* like—and begin to live out *your* dreams.

What if you could feel that same level of freedom and energy almost every day of your life?

You can. We all can. Instead of channeling that energy into carrying around a 100-pound pack, feeling like a prisoner in our own life, we can use it to move purposefully toward the better, more meaningful expression we're meant for.

If we only know how.

Rediscovering the Fire in You

Whenever I think about Real Rule #4, I think of Joe, one of my coaching clients and heroes. Joe awoke one morning to an unspeakable nightmare, one that would put his heart in a coma for many years.

Joe's daughter, Jessica, was a remarkable young woman who had just finished training to become a dental assistant. Her best friend was in an extremely abusive live-in relationship, and Jessica was determined to help her get out of a dangerous situation. So one day, she went to her girlfriend's house and helped her pack up all her stuff.

On their way out, the boyfriend arrived home. He saw what Jessica was doing, and he told her, "You're dead." That night, he broke into her apartment and murdered her. Joe was at his home when he got the call from the police.

For several years, as they searched for Jessica's killer, it was a struggle for Joe just to want to stay alive. In many ways, he was punishing himself. Because his daughter had been robbed of her life, Joe felt the need to sacrifice a part of his life, too. His friends reached out to him, but he had absolutely no desire to go out for a great steak dinner or play 18 holes of golf with the guys. How could he even think of enjoying his life when his daughter had lost hers?

Friends and family tried to bring Joe back into life, but it felt like sacrilege for him to go on living when Jessica didn't have that chance. Consumed by pain and rage, he lost his appetite for living and lapsed into what I call a "grief coma."

Is survivor's guilt real? You bet it is. Especially for parents who outlive their children. Living with nonproductive emotions such as guilt can suck the energy right out of our lives. But it's not only guilt that keeps us from moving forward after a tragedy; it's the feeling of undeservedness. At the core, Joe didn't feel as though he deserved to go on with his life when his daughter's had ended so tragically. As a parent, you sign on as the guardian of your child's life, and that never stops. Even though it was totally irrational, Joe couldn't stop blaming himself for his daughter's death. Somehow, some way, he felt he should have been able to save her from this horrible fate. And was punishing himself uncontrollably with blame.

I spoke to Joe almost every day for several years, father to father. And, slowly but surely, he began to get a handle on what it would mean to come alive again. We'd meet every few weeks at a Carl's Jr. midway between our houses for a ½-pound burger and a Diet Coke. And we'd talk. Sometimes we would even laugh. It was a start. Joe even agreed to go on a motorcycle trip through the Swiss Alps with a few buddies. Things did not look good the first day as tears streamed down his face. Perhaps he had made a terrible mistake traveling so far from the comfort of his home. But on the second day of the trip as they drove through breathtaking mountain pastures, something began to shift. "It was like suddenly I could take a deep, deep breath, all the way into the lower part of my lungs," he later explained. Letting go of his tears on the first day, clearing some of his pain, had made space for life. Joe's energy had been tied up in feeling guilt, rage, blame, and undeservedness. He could begin to breathe again.

Getting Real—"The Power of Breath"

It's no coincidence that Joe described the key shift in his healing as taking a deep breath. The natural process of breathing ties us to the true core of who we are; the more deeply we breathe, the more connected we are to both our honest self and the world around us. This is why practices like yoga and meditation focus so intently on the breath for creating spaciousness and restoring vitality.

Joe has continued to make space in his heart for the side of life that is not pain, where he can experience some measure of peace and enjoyment. Today he is fighting the good fight. He has stopped running from reality and found ways to process all the emotions surrounding his daughter's death. Especially the self-inflicted blame. This has made all the difference. He has tapped a new source of energy and it shows. We joke around a lot more when we get together and even play a round of golf once in a while. Joe has slowly opened himself up to life again. He still cries once in a while thinking about his beautiful Jessica and how much he misses her. And this will probably never change. But he has successfully fought his way back into life. And he is breathing again. Joe is truly one of my heroes. As he puts it, "I've got some fire in me again, Brother Ken!"

Where is energy tied up in your life? What relationship or situation might be sucking life out of you? That bolt of new energy may be a step away, or a thank you away, an apology away, or a kind word to yourself away . . . but it's probably not as far away as you might think. And now is the perfect time to begin doing what is necessary to set yourself free.

Doing an *energy audit* on yourself might precipitate some important awareness and possibly some profound changes. Clear your slate of paralyzing guilt, fear, blame, and admonitions and reignite the fire within.

Real Action

RR#4 TAKEAWAYS

Sometimes it's difficult to know where energy is tied up in our lives because we're so accustomed to carrying around that 100-pound pack. Take a moment to do an energy audit on yourself: what is sapping your time and energy?

EXERCISE #1 Check the time-and-energy sucks that are robbing you.

❑ A draining relationship or job

❑ Feelings of guilt or undeservedness

❑ Fear of either ending or confronting a relationship

❑ Feelings of low self-esteem and low self-worth that keep you down

---

❏ A social calendar or activity list that's depleting you

❏ Being chronically overcommitted at school or work

❏ Spending too much time and energy on the Internet (or computer, or smartphone)

EXERCISE #2 Identifying the energy- and time-drains in your life is only half the battle. Once you've got an idea of the problem areas, list three things you can do to begin freeing yourself from each one.

EXERCISE #3 Write yourself a letter explaining what it would mean to free up/unburden your time, energy, heart, and life. Tell yourself what you will do to change in the next six months. Open and read the letter in six months.

EXERCISE #4 List 25 things that give you energy, like getting a great hug, going horseback riding, relaxing in front of the fireplace, working in the garden, reading a great book, taking a bath, journaling, being held, etc.

Real Rule #5

LIFE IS DESIGNED TO BREAK YOUR HEART:
Managing Love and Intimacy

Heartbreak gets an awfully bad rap.

Sounds like I've gone off the deep end, right? After all, we spend our whole lives trying desperately to avoid heartbreak, disapproval, and rejection, for all the obvious reasons. It hurts. It's miserable. Why would anyone ever stick up for heartbreak?

If we don't take risks in life and love, or invest anything of our hearts, then what do you predict we will have at the end of our lives? Will we be nothing but empty husks with little of real value to show for our time on the planet? Will we be safe, fat, and happy? Maybe we'll have no great losses to report . . . but only because we took no risks. Will our hearts look as perfect as a 1967 Corvette that's been "garaged" for 45 years—because we had no great loves to scratch the paint? Or the '67 'Vette that's got over 100,000 miles, a few scratches, a few dents, and thousands of memories?

It's Real Rule #5: Life Is Designed to Break Your Heart.

If life is made up of trade-offs, then one of the most wonderful and perplexing is love. People who live the richest, most fulfilling lives are the ones who open their hearts to love. They're also the ones who are likely going to experience heartbreak, separation, and loss. Life doesn't go on forever; neither do relationships. Someday, in some way, you will lose those you love.

And I'm not just talking about romantic love. I'm talking about the love parents have for their children and the love children have for their parents. I'm talking about love between brothers, sisters, cousins, and best friends. Army buddies and teammates. Love grips us in many forms. But every relationship demands the same thing from us: that we open ourselves to the other person, are vulnerable, and show them our true selves—all with the risk that we could lose them at any moment.

A broken heart is not a bad thing. Brokenness is a measure of the heart that has given of itself generously—not foolishly as often thought. We all want our hearts to be full at the end of our lives.

Picture in your mind someone doing a psychological autopsy of a heart that protected itself and held back, spending its entire lifetime encased in protection like the 1967 Corvette. Not only does it have hardened arteries—the whole thing is walled up, surrounded by fear-based excuses, rationalizations, explanations, and justifications. Remember those diagrams of smokers' lungs from your seventh grade health book? The closed heart looks like that, only worse. Black and decaying—not much to show there.

Now imagine doing the same autopsy on a heart that lived fully! A heart that opened, that made room, that learned how to be authentic, constantly increasing its capacity for love. And yes, that heart probably experienced the great anguish and pain that come with the territory of being a human who takes risks. If you're a person who opens your heart and takes risks loving people, you're going to get hurt sooner or later. It's one of life's package deals. Put your heart on the line, give of your love generously and receive it graciously, and you will experience the best life has to offer. You'll likely experience a heartbreak or two along the way, but the rewards will be worth it.

Back to your imaginary heart. You want the folks doing the heart autopsy to say, "Look at this! This heart loved so fully. It really gave everything it had. All the love, the gratitude, the appreciation, the affection—

it was all given away. But not only that. Look here, it also received a lot of love—which explains why it looks so full. If we wanted to find the love that started here, we'd find it in the smiles and memories of all the people who were touched by this heart, because now it lives within them."

Getting Real—"The Used-Up Heart"

It may sound harsh to celebrate a "used-up" heart. But a heart isn't like fossil fuel. There's no limited supply. The more you use it, the more love is created, and the more gifts you receive. Remember, the heart is a muscle. The more it's flexed, the stronger it becomes.

Risking It All

What could be better than the feeling of being loved and of loving in return? It's like soaring to the very top of the world. The feeling may arise at the sight of your newborn baby (holding my daughters for the first time were two of the happiest moments of my life), in a moment of blissful connection with a life partner, or at the 89th birthday party of an ailing mother (like my own) whose love has only grown deeper each year since she gave birth to you.

Anyone who's ever felt it knows that love lifts us up and makes us more alive. And yet, no matter how much we love another person, we can't deny the fact that eventually, they'll be lost to us. And yet, we must take the risk. Whether by death or another cause, all our earthly relationships someday come to an end.

"Living losses"—to divorce or separation, estrangement, illness, or incapacitation—can be the hardest of all. Distraught parents tell me, "I'm estranged from my son," or "My daughter has been missing for two months." They suffer the agony of not knowing. And yet for many parents, including my friend Beth Holloway (whose daughter, Natalee, went missing in Aruba several years ago), sensing that their child may be gone or suffering—is excruciating. I think of all the 9/11 families I worked with who waited and waited for confirmation of what they already knew in their hearts. Their greatest hope was that the authorities would find some DNA so that they could finally put their loved one to rest. The waiting, the not knowing—these living losses are gaping wounds that take an eternity to even begin healing.

If the pain of loss is so crushing, so totally devastating, why risk loving at all?

Some of us choose not to take the risk. Maybe life has already been too painful. Or perhaps the people who were supposed to love us—our parents, other relatives, and spouse—betrayed our trust.

The love (or lack thereof) we felt as kids affects how we open our hearts as adults. We each have ways of protecting ourselves as we navigate our way in the world, and what we're navigating, most of the time, is love and intimacy. "How safe is it?" we ask ourselves, consciously or subconsciously, every time we are invited to embark upon, or go deeper into a relationship. How safe is it for me to get closer? To really show this person who I am? To entrust my heart to them?

Creating safety and intimacy in our relationships are things that take a lifetime to master. Sharing our lives, dreams, and hearts with another person is the dance of intimacy. And we're all making it up as we go. Sometimes we struggle, stepping on each other's toes, and sometimes we soar. Sometimes we give of ourselves in loving and selfless ways and the best in us comes out. And sometimes something happens that brings out the very worst in us, and we become cold and selfish.

One of the biggest mistakes couples make is to play it safe. Going through the motions, playing it safe by risking little or nothing of consequence, we tell ourselves that we have nothing to lose. Right? Withholding our innermost needs and feelings from our partner or family, fearing we'll only make things worse by speaking our hearts, is risky business. Not only does silence deaden our relationships, it robs us of the intimacy that connects us so dearly to those we love. When the debt finally comes due (as it always does), and the floodgates open, we discover how wrong we were. Faking it, investing nothing, and thinking we can hide the truth forever, is a formula for disaster.

It goes without saying that "marriages of convenience" a.
to mediocrity. Or worse. To be in true partnership with another hu.
being, we must construct our relationship on what's real, not on smoke
and mirrors. Or all the appearances of intimacy, myths and "fillers" we
use in the absence of true intimacy. Intimacy is built on what is authentic and real—on being truly who you are.

Getting Real—"The Remedy for Love"

As Henry David Thoreau once said, "There is no remedy for
love but to love more."

In order to open ourselves up in this way and to love, we have to
take risks. Allowing yourself to be known, truly known, by another human being requires courage. To dare to really know and merge with another person and blend our life with theirs means we must risk our very
hearts. Loving deeply can be one of the most treacherous or uplifting
experiences we can have in this life. To-have loved, be it our children,
parents, partners, or friends, makes life richer and grows our souls. In
the grand scheme of things, to have loved is perhaps the greatest and
most honorable risk we could ever take.

A Smart Heart

Going out into the world and making good decisions with people
who are loving, responsible, and trustworthy is a lot different than going out and making foolish decisions with people who are inauthentic
and reckless with our hearts. Those people have not earned our trust.
That's why Real Rule #5 comes with a caveat: it's up to you to take smart
risks with love. You don't want to put your heart in the care of anybody
who's going to hide their true self, treat you poorly, and/or turn out to
be psychologically unavailable. Trust must be earned and renewed regularly by our actions.

Getting Real—"Loving Smart"

Relationships are spiritual paths. Like any great spiritual path, they are rife with ruts, potholes, and challenges. Taking smart risks with love means being wary of the dangers and obstacles while also maintaining an open, loving heart.

Even if we do choose wisely, love can make us do crazy things. It can make us blind. We can all identify at least several silly or even stupid things we did, or failed to do, because of love and infatuation. Our hearts are singing and we're skipping along through fields of daffodils, because we see in our new love all the things we've been dreaming of. We're about to attain all we've ever wanted. Right?

Maybe we are, maybe we aren't. Our dreams might come true, and they might not. Either way, take a moment to step back at the beginning of every new relationship and assess the risks. Are you being smart? Do you really know this person? Have you been 100 percent honest? Are you making wise decisions? Is there anything he or she is doing that you're whitewashing (i.e., making excuses for, rationalizing, justifying, or defending)? If so, it's time to be strong and get real with yourself! Respectfully communicate your concerns to the other person. And let the cards fall where they may.

In the context of an already existing relationship, being smart is all the more important. Relationships aren't just casual links with other people. They're a living spiritual path. There's nothing more revealing, humiliating, uplifting, and humbling than being in an intimate relationship with another human being. Nothing in the world will push us to grow more. Relationships are where all our "young parts" eventually show up. All our walls of protection are going to be challenged to come down, and who we truly are is going to be called out, one way or another. We can go willingly, or we can go kicking and screaming.

Obviously, the opportunity to grow on this spiritual path is huge. I encourage couples to do whatever is necessary to face into and "push through" the barriers to intimacy. Communication is the key. If an issue shows up in your relationship, talk about it! Perfect the art of talking things out in all your relationships. Working it through is the only hope for "breaking through" to a higher and better expression of who you are—and developing a more intimate, loving, trustworthy, and truly generous side of yourself. Only then can we transcend the fears that may have formed a crusty protective shell over our heart.

Initially our fears are there in service to our survival, but now they may be threatening it. We have to know the point at which our own defenses begin to diminish our capacity for love and even compromise our safety. That's when we must find healthier, stronger, more effective ways of protecting ourselves that don't disallow or inhibit closeness. Like making excuses for, or justifying, the behavior of your partner rather than calling them on it.

One of the best ways to grow closer is to simply own up to things with your partner. Stop playing games and be truthful, even when it's hard. As Swiss psychiatrist Carl Jung so eloquently pointed out, each of us has a "shadow" side—the small part of us that gets scared, jealous, and arrogant. The shadow is the side of our nature that we're a bit embarrassed (or even ashamed) about. We try to hide, deny, repress, and avoid it, pretending it doesn't exist.

However, all the shadow confirms is that we're human. We all have a darker side. The trick is learning how to harness the power of the shadow by becoming aware of and owning it, instead of trying to hide it because we're ashamed. And what better place to do that than in open exchanges with your partner, who is simultaneously striving to become aware of and contain his or her shadow side as well? Allowing love or ambition to blind you to the shadow side of someone you're looking to build a future with will surely come back to bite you in the butt. The choice is simple: get a handle on your shadow feelings—your own and those of your loved ones—or they'll get a handle on you.

Getting Real—"The Shadow Side"

The shadow side is endemic to the human condition. It's home to the less-than-ideal parts of ourselves. We all have a shadow. There are no exceptions. Harnessing the power of our shadow begins with owning up to the "scared, small" part of ourselves. By owning up to it, we contain it. This kind of transparency and humility opens and frees us.

Years ago, at the tail end of a fairly extensive media tour to promote my first book, after an endless marathon of book signings, workshops, and readings, I called my wife.

"I've been on the road for three weeks," I told her, "and I'll be coming home in a few days. I want to ease my way back into the family—and right now I am exhausted. Empty. I'm going to come through that door with very little to give. I am calling because I wanted to prepare you, because I'm about to fall through the front door broken, exhausted, and needy, not knowing if all this running around really accomplished anything. That's who's coming home."

My wife thanked me for warning her of my "condition." By being totally honest with her, I gave her the information she needed to take good care of herself—and our relationship. While I "vegged" in bed for a few days, she was able to take care of herself, the kids, and me. It's this sort of proactive, preventive communication that enables us to use our shadow to get *closer* to our partner, no matter what shape we're in.

No matter how smart we are about the risks we take, loving still inevitably opens us up to change. It's in the nature of life to do so. At the end of our lives, don't we want our hearts to be the perfect proof that we loved and loved well? And grew our souls?

While a heart that has been broken may ache like no other, it is one that has dared to love without condition and to take smart risks. As

20th-century poet Rainer Maria Rilke said so eloquently, the heart that is "never exposed to loss, innocent and secure, cannot know tenderness; only the won-back heart can ever be satisfied: free, through all it has given up, to rejoice in its mastery." There is no greater testament to a life well-lived than a heart that got its full measure of use.

Real Action

RR#5 TAKEAWAYS

Love is one of the great human journeys. There was and is great love behind every heartbreak. That's what it's all about, this messy thing we call life: our hearts overflowing with love one moment, and breaking in two the next.

EXERCISES #1 While none of us is immune to heartbreak, it's our responsibility to take smart risks and make smart choices when it comes to loving those around us. Here are some doable ways to love richly and well. Check the ones you most need to remind yourself about.

❏ When you're in a loving relationship, give of yourself fearlessly.

❏ Always get to know someone before you trust them with your heart.

❏ Practice ways of demonstrating your love to friends, family, and partners in the love languages that speak to them (physical affection, time spent together, gifts, etc.).

❏ If and when heartbreak strikes, be gentle with yourself and remember that it is better to have loved fully and courageously than not at all.

EXERCISE #2 Name a few of your "shadow" feelings. Summon the courage to share them with your partner, a close family member, or a friend as a gesture of your intent to become more transparent, intimate, and trustworthy.

Real Rule #6

IT IS WHAT IT IS:
Dancing with Reality

---

*"*It's all good." We hear it all the time—from family members, friends, politicians, and talk show hosts who are at a loss to explain why things unfold the way they do or what we can do about them. In 2004, *USA Today* voted it the "Sports Quote" of the year. But the days of "It's all good" have come to an end. In its place, we have: "It is what it is."

It may seem like a cliché. Some might argue that it's a trite, convenient way to elude all personal responsibility or to blow past all the heartache and frustration that comes from loss and other forms of adversity. But if we push past the fact that the phrase is suffering from serious overuse, we see that it's actually a very profound thing to be able to say. So important that it deserves a spot in the Real Rules of Life.

The "is what it is" statement implies a tacit acknowledgment that, even if you don't understand what "it" is, it is what it is regardless. It's a proclamation that life has its own terms, and while we naturally get to set some of our own, it's still going to turn out the way it turns out. It's our job to "balance the books"—to reconcile life's debts and gains, assets and losses, suffering and joy. As we have said, so much of what transpires in this life is beyond our comprehension and our control. It is . . . what it is.

To believe the opposite (i.e., "It is what I say it is") is dangerous and misleading, because it means operating with righteous certainty. The person who refuses to believe "It is what it is" says, "I know what it is. So I'm going to tell you what it is, and that's all there is to it." What follows is typically some "irrefutable" doctrine or rigidly held religious, political, or philosophic belief that the person claims to be absolute truth.

I'm not against politics, philosophy, or religion. So many great things have happened in the name of faith-based organizations—service, honor, and allegiance; loving and cherishing and a code for living a rich life and embracing that which is greater than all of us. What I am against is any belief system that claims to be the sole and exclusive owner of what is real and authentic. It is that kind of self-righteous, superior approach to life that not only divides people around the world, but divides us internally. It drives a wedge between us and within us.

When a rigidly held belief is claimed as truth, where there is no humility, we polarize into groups. Fundamentalists from any creed believe, "I hold the leasehold and the copyright to the truth, and you don't. So I'm going to impose my truth on you." It also happens in psychology, law—you name it. These are the places where our arrogance still gets us into trouble with each other, the world, and even ourselves.

When people hold their beliefs with humility, belief stops being a dividing factor and becomes a gift. The shift from "I know" to "This is how I understand it" sometimes makes the difference between war and peace. It says "There also might be another way of seeing it." It acknowledges, "Maybe I don't have all the answers." And it reassures that "If you choose a different path, I will do my very best to understand and respect it."

Some people are surprised to learn that there's a common "disclaimer" embedded in almost every faith: humility. The Baha'is call God "the unknowable essence." What a gentle and poetic rendering of the limitations we all face.

And the Baha'is are not alone. Tucked within the folds of every great religious tradition is a humble respect for what is ultimately true: that none of us is a perfect vessel of truth or understanding. We are all learning as we go.

As wise as we might become, as spiritually aligned as we feel, as tuned in to nature and the universe as we may be, we're still part of a great mystery. No tradition—religious or philosophical, spiritual or scientific—can consider itself complete unless it acknowledges that mystery unfolding. The same goes for any individual, including professional clergy, gurus, mediums, psychologists, authors, nonbelievers, and/or New Age teachers. There has to be a self-educating, self-policing humility that states: "My thinking is partial and incomplete. I'm reflecting on the part of the truth that I've come to understand, but I'm open to continued discovery." In other words: "I'm a work in progress, and my understanding of myself, God, and the universe is also a work in progress."

Getting Real—"The Beauty of Paradox"

It's often said that paradox is the highest form of truth. The beauty of paradox is that it allows us to touch into life's deeper understandings. When we try to make it one way or the other, we lose something in the translation.

Real Rule #6 reminds us that life is as much a process of knowing and understanding as it is of not knowing and not understanding. "It is what it is" is a humble invitation to explore, not a resignation to ignorance. Close-mindedness breeds fear, hostility, disconnection, and even violence, while this kind of openness forges a path to peace, humility, and understanding.

An Open Door

There's a simple concept that's read at the end of AA meetings all over the world. I affectionately call it "The Humility Prayer" and it goes like this: "We realize we know only a little. More will be revealed to you and to us."

AA's *Big Book* is full of equally beautiful pieces of humble wisdom. That there are many paths to God. That faith is as much a mystery as anything else. That our diversity and creativity allow us to custom-design our faith to fit the real circumstances of our life. For me, these tenets are the embodiment of real wisdom, real sacredness. What is unholy is to say: "This is the truth about God, and only I possess it. You have to conform to it or else."

Take, for example, the fundamentalist theory that the 2010 earthquake in Haiti happened because the Haitians turned against Christ 200 years ago and embraced voodoo. A number of prominent Christian leaders rejected this theory outright, but it, and others like it, continue to float around many circles and are endorsed publicly by leading televangelists.

Such views are not only dangerous; they're reckless and exploitative. They're a product of people who use the tragedies and misfortunes of others to promote their own agenda. Using the Haiti earthquake or any natural disaster to aggrandize one's own belief system by skewing it into a sobering example of "how the world works" is sacrilege. There's no humility there, and certainly no sensitivity. Not very "Christlike," either.

Blaming the victim is as old as time. Why? Because frightened human beings cling so desperately to being right. Rather than give up their belief system, they try to fit all that is tragic, horrible, and senseless—or at the other end of the spectrum, all of life's blessings—into their personal schema. They have to interpret these events in a way that serves their beliefs as they've constructed them. "Would a just God take the lives of 230,000 people, injure 300,000, and render 1,000,000 homeless?" they ask. "Surely not. Then the Haitians must have done something to deserve this fate. It must be the hand of justice that we simply can't see."

Mired in Spin

The world is full of spinmeisters of bad news. Flip through your TV channels and you'll spot them all over the place. They're there to show us how to justify great losses—how to put a shiny bow on life's tragedies.

These losses become lessons, ways of teaching us how we should be living or what we should believe in. Instead of allowing the hard parts of life to simply be hard, people want to use them to reinforce the sanctity of their belief system, to justify its existence and to "sell" it to a larger audience.

Consider the group of Orthodox Jews who believe that the reason the epicenter of the Holocaust was in Germany is because that's where reform Judaism came into existence a century earlier. In every faith, there tends to be great internal tension between the orthodox believers and the reformers. Instead of embracing the differences, people look at each other with arrogant superiority and harsh judgment. Each side believes they've got it right; that they are the sole possessors of Truth with a capital T. Ironically, nothing could be *further* from the truth.

There's a line from the Talmud (the Jewish book of ethics, law, history, customs, and philosophy) that reads, "Do not make the Torah into a crown with which to aggrandize yourself or as a spade with which to dig."

What that piece of wisdom means to me is that the Torah, or any religious book, is ours to study and to master, but we must hold its teachings in gentle hands. Judaism, like any other religion, is not a "sales" tool for us to market.

Getting Real—"The Gift of Religion"

People who use religion as an excuse to spread judgment and hatred, and to exert power, are denying one of its most honorable purposes: as a source of wisdom. True wisdom and faith are gifts that help us wrap our hearts and minds around all of life's unknowns.

We can't force-feed our faith to others. We must hold the wisdom in a way that allows us to grow and deepen our understanding of ourselves and one another, instead of using it to lay claim to the truth. We must graciously and humbly invite others into the wealth of our faith, strength, wisdom, and codes for living.

The name of God used in the Bible is often mistranslated as "I am what I am." The actual Hebrew translation is "I will be what I will be." In other words, God holds the right to alter his or her Beingness as the situation demands. Think of how different (safer, more just, compassionate, and connected) a place the world would be if we became just as flexible in our understanding of what the "truth" is.

The most holy approaches to faith don't slam doors in people's faces. Rather, they open them unto life's great mystery . . . and beckon us in. When it comes to the "It is what it is" take on life, let's also remember that, "It is what we make it."

Real Action

RR#6 TAKEAWAYS

Accepting that "it is what it is" requires stepping into the dance of reality—a dance where it's impossible to know and understand everything.

Where do you stand on the "It is what it is" issue?

EXERCISE #1 On a scale from 1 to 10, how tightly do you hold onto your faith/beliefs as superior to that of others?

EXERCISE #2 Are there certain beliefs that you hold rigidly in your heart? List them. Next to each one, write down a benefit of loosening your grip a little.

EXERCISE #3 Check the items below that might help you become more humble without compromising what you have chosen to believe in.

- ❏ Go to a religious service that is different from yours and make it a point to find several things there that you consider to be holy.

- ❏ Try listening to someone whose belief system you don't agree with. Listen for the ways their beliefs are similar to yours. Write down a few of the common threads.

Real Rule #7

THERE ARE NO QUICK FIXES:
It Takes What It Takes to Mend

Not long ago, I was standing in a hot gymnasium, preparing to give a speech to 3,000 high school students who had watched 13 of their peers die in the prior year.

I wasn't back at Columbine High School. I was in Oceanside, California.

This high school wasn't one of the ones people knew about—it hadn't caused a media sensation; it hadn't been plastered all over CNN and NBC. But in just one year, they had lost 13 students to suicide, homicides, car accidents, and cancer. Their guidance counselor, a buddy of mine, called me up and asked me to speak to the student body. "These kids are really struggling, Ken. Would you please come and talk to them?"

That night, I put together a talk called "Life Lessons from Grief." Standing before 3,000 high school students sweating in the gymnasium the following day, I opened with an apology.

"I want to give you the same apology I gave to both of my daughters thirteen years ago," I said. "My generation has given you the impression that there is a pill for every pain, a distraction for every emptiness, a fix for every problem. And it's not the truth.

"The reality is that some things are unfixable in life and that sometimes, things just really suck. When we lose someone we love, it's natural to feel sad, angry, and confused. We look for the remote control because we want to change the channel or hit the rewind button. We wish we could just step into a time machine and go back to the way it used to be, and to 'undo' what happened. But life doesn't work that way, does it?

"You lost thirteen of your classmates this year, and that sucks. Big time. I wouldn't blame you if you wanted to numb out with TV or a video game. Drone out reality with noise and music and schoolwork and nonstop activity. These are all things that most adults have tried. The problem is that they aren't effective. As a matter of fact, they make things even worse. I don't blame you for feeling the way you feel. How could you not feel all these things? And how could you not just want to block all this out, hoping it will go away and things will somehow magically get better?"

I went on to talk about what it really means to be a human being—and that there are times in every person's life when we need to muster every ounce of strength we have just to get through it. I also talked about how the school community needed to work hard to become a safe place. Not just a place free of weapons, gangs, drunken drivers, and bullies, but a place where students could talk openly and honestly about their pain and sorrow. A place where students weren't told to "just get over it" and "get back to class," but were allowed to feel sadness, anger, confusion, and fear with no timelines attached. Where they were given the support they really *needed* to go on.

That advice goes for all of us. It's up to us to become the kind of parents, friends, and co-workers who make it safe for those around us to "process" emotions like grief. Spoon-feeding our friends and colleagues with clichés, spin, and dogma doesn't help anybody. We need to stand with them in whatever they feel. Instead of trying to make it all better, we've got to acknowledge Real Rule #7: There Are No Quick Fixes.

The Bad Rap on Touchy-Feely

My friend Jim's eight-year-old daughter, Carley, is suffering from inoperable brain cancer. Jim has spent far too many evenings sitting vigil outside the emergency room with his family, waiting for the doctors to come out and tell them Carley is going to be all right. The anguish and anxiety of these terrifying trips to the ER are intolerable. And Jim catches himself taking it out on the hospital staff.

After a tearful, sobbing "meltdown" with the family doctor, who is an old, dear friend, Jim realized he had really needed a good cry for quite some time. Releasing what had been building up inside of him gave Jim the strength and clarity to request a much-needed meeting with his daughter's pediatric oncologist. The game plan that came out of that meeting has given Jim new confidence and strength to move forward. He is no longer biting his tongue, having to stop himself from offering the doctors and nurses unsolicited advice, challenging their approach, telling them how they could be handling things better. No longer is he allowing the fear of losing his daughter—and his anger about her condition—to build up inside of him. "Why is it always so hard for me to just accept how I feel? Of course I'm scared. Of course I feel helpless. How else should I feel?" he shared.

Our tolerance for certain emotions, like helplessness and fear, is minimal. It's hard for us to deal with the raw pain of threat and loss, because we're just not equipped to handle it. Or to cope. That's why we try to figure out, fix, and put a spin on things. Or, alternatively, to hold it all inside.

The modern notion that we can become masters of our own destiny—setting our minds on a course for "success" using techniques like visualization and positive affirmations—has been empowering, to say the least. Stories of self-directed entrepreneurs abound. But the idea that we can control everything this way has given rise to a disturbing tendency—that of trying to squash "negative" emotions. We especially hate feeling helpless. Our kids grow up being told to sit quietly at their desks with their hands folded. We don't give them constructive outlets for their rage and anger, confusion, curiosity, and sorrow.

Instead, when certain emotions pop up on the radar screen, we play shoot the messenger. We crucify those feelings of sorrow or fury. They're just not allowed. We push them away in our attempts to move on. But emotions are simply radar signals. Even if what you're feeling is unsettling or uncomfortable, be thankful you can feel emotion—it's proof that you're alive!

Instead of shooting the messenger, we've got to listen to the message and understand what we might be trying to show or tell ourselves. Sorrow may be there to show me how much I really cared about someone. Confusion, to tell me how inadequate my understanding of the world has been. And now these feelings are pushing me open to a greater, deeper understanding—and often into action. There's nothing wrong with you. Your equipment is working just fine. In fact it is a wonderfully reassuring, life-affirming thing to be able to feel.

Somewhere along the line, we've gotten the notion that feelings are bad. Think of all the negative press they've gotten. Nobody wants to be described as "soft" or "touchy-feely," because presumably, "touching" and "feeling" are indulgent, excessive, weak, and unnecessary. They make us appear vulnerable and inept. So we've tried to think our way through and around things—to prove ourselves in control and rational beings. In the aftermath of the Enlightenment, intellect is prized above all else, including our most human emotions.

Getting Real—"Instant Messaging"

We may think of IMing as something that happens exclusively in a virtual realm. But when we experience a negative or traumatic event, it registers on our very real emotional landscape. More often than not, we choose to ignore these instant emotional messages. Yet noticing them is crucial to awareness, decision making, learning, and healing.

The "positive" psychology that's currently so popular gives people the impression that they can positive-think their way through or around any bad feeling or experience. What they're really doing is repressing feelings that do exist. The feeling either comes back stronger than before, or it has to become a crusted-over, incorporated, deeply hidden secret that we carry around behind a badge of shame.

"We don't always have a choice about what happens in our lives, or about the pain that inescapably accompanies loss, do we?" I asked the kids at El Camino High School. They didn't have a say as to whether or not their 13 friends died. "But we do have a choice," I told them, "about expressing our tears and sorrow, about doing things that really help us heal, about honoring and remembering our friends, and about learning the life lessons from grief."

We know very little about what our universe is, where it's all going, or where it came from. Just as we know little about how to fill the absence of the classmate, co-worker, or innocence we lost. Not only can we not figure it out or fix it, we shouldn't try. The harder we try to make sense of what doesn't make sense, the further away from ourselves we wander, the more disembodied, disassociated, disconnected, and desensitized we become.

Being With

When we're out of touch with our own emotions, when we're "in our heads," it's difficult to relate to someone else's feelings. To empathize. That's why we so often feel like we have to put a bow (i.e., positive spin) on other people's hardships and losses. Why we try to figure them out and fix them. Why it's so uncomfortable for us to hear what someone else is feeling when they're going through a rough time. And why it's sometimes easier to pretend things are okay when they're not.

We have not learned how to cope very well. "If it were me who lost a spouse or got fired or no longer had a home, then I'd feel helpless, and very, very sad," we tell ourselves. And that's too scary. So instead of putting ourselves in someone else's shoes, feeling what they're going through, listening, and empathizing, we try for a quick fix. Most often, ans "projecting" our own fears onto the situation, trying to explain away and fix things with oversimplified remedies, heroically trying to rescue the other person (as though they were a helpless victim), and/or doing something radical (such as taking them to Vegas) to take their minds off of their problem. Projection, much like rationalization and justification—two other widely used defense mechanisms—is designed to "protect" us from the hard-to-swallow truth about ourselves. Casting blame, motives, and attributions onto others, whether we're consciously aware of it or not, redirects the shame, guilt, and responsibility we feel away from ourselves. We may even begin to believe our own untruths, carrying us further and further away from our true selves and others.

So if we're more honest with ourselves and acknowledge Real Rule #7—that there are no quick fixes—then what's the alternative? Once we stop trying to fix or put a spin on loss, what could and should we do instead?

The answer is simple: be with.

When Jenna was a little girl, she used to call to me, "Daddy, come be with." What she meant was, "Come over here and just keep me company, Dad. Don't try to fix me or get distracted."

For me, "being with" meant turning down the noise in my own head. Noise that was telling me I had too many other things to do, or that I had to be a perfect father—to fix this and solve that. With all that noise playing, we never really get to hear our child or spouse. We're too busy figuring it all out, rehearsing the shorthand responses we think will make that person feel better, take away their pain, make them more comfortable . . . and so on. When, in truth, those responses are probably not what they're asking for, or what they need.

Getting Real—"Being With"

"Being with" means to be a quiet, healing presence. To really listen. And care. It doesn't require that you do anything. It simply means bearing witness to what another human being is going through.

Our best moments as parents, spouses, co-workers, and friends are undoubtedly the ones when we listen with grace. Listen, rather than project our own fears or helplessness into the situation, or impose our own need to fix things and take away their suffering. When we just show up, it makes all the difference.

I did hundreds of interviews for my book *How to Talk to Your Kids About School Violence*. The title originated from the most common questions parents asked me, like: "How *do* I talk to my kids?" My most common answer was: "The best way to talk to your kids is not to talk—but to listen."

The sign of a truly respectful, attentive, wise parent is that they have a lot of scar tissue on the tip of their tongue from all the times they've had to bite it. It's in our nature to want to fix our kids. To take away their pain and stress. We're like functional engineers: "Figure it out and fix it." We want to take away anything "bad" our kids may be feeling. In so doing, we often treat them as helpless.

But the more you play "Daddy Fix-it," the more dependent your kids become. The refrain becomes: "Mom, Dad, I don't know what to do! Fix this for me! Give me the answer!" You become the pusher: the supplier of quick fixes. When, as Real Rule #7 says, there is no such thing.

The best thing we can possibly do for our kids is to draw them out with respectful open-ended questions—and to listen well. These questions don't have a hidden message. "Did you actually forget your homework again?" doesn't count. That's not a question; that's an accusatory statement disguised as a question. Truly open-ended questions are a welcoming invitation that asks: "How did you feel about that? What do you think you should do?" When your child responds, make your first response to reflect back to them what they've said so they know you were really listening. It's about being an attentive witness—and a calm, clear presence—not running around in a panic with your hair on fire or rescuing them because they're helpless.

This doesn't apply just to parents. It goes for any relationship—employees, friends, your spouse. Being a good listener and asking open-ended questions helps the other person think about their options. They'll be better equipped to make good decisions on their own behalf.

It fosters independence and empowers the people around you, rather than calling attention to you and continuing to make others dependent on you.

Honor your children and employees and friends. And yourself. Draw them out with open-ended questions. Bite your tongue when necessary. Listen intimately. Reflect back to them exactly what they are saying, as much as is humanly possible, so they know they have been heard. Help them consider and assess their feelings—not judging or trying to change how they feel. Once they see you care, chances are that your feelings will be received with the same patience, understanding, and respect. Doing unto others as we would have them do unto us is truly the "Golden" rule when it comes to *being with*.

There really is no better way to show our love than to listen attentively. Which brings us to Real Rule #8: Listening Is Love.

Real Action

RR#7 TAKEAWAYS

Whatever form of adversity you're suffering, whatever the nature of your biggest challenge, healing is a slow and uneven process. It will take what it will take to mend your heart. Whatever time. Whatever support. This is also true for the people in your life who are dealing with adversity. There are no quick fixes, no magic pills, and no shortcuts. As tempting as it can be to want to "fix" yourself or your loved ones, doing so circumvents the natural healing process.

EXERCISE #1 Do you sense in yourself a tendency to want to be a rescuer or "fixer"? If the answer is yes, pick one of these simple approaches to "being with" and empowering others:

- The next time someone comes to me with a problem or heartbreak, I will resist the urge to solve it and just be an attentive listener.

- I will practice the art of silence and listening without judgment, believing in, and encouraging others to implement their own best solutions.

- When I am struggling, I will breathe through the pain, remember that healing is a process, and take all the time I need.

EXERCISE #2 Can you think of anybody you're "projecting" onto? If so, what would it take for you to stop and deal with them in a more direct manner?

EXERCISE #3 List five important people in your life. Next to each name, write down what you could do to really "be with" them in the future.

Real Rule #8

LISTENING IS LOVE:
How to Really Listen To Strengthen Relationships

Who ever heard of taking a class in listening? Probably very few of us! But listening is an incredible thing. It's how we communicate our most basic needs and how we connect with others.

Language is a conduit to both our inner and outer world. But while meaning is flowing out when we speak, meaning is also flowing in when we listen. We use language as a way to represent ourselves and forge connections with others, but we also use it to feel understood. Effective communication is about forming my words to transmit meaning to you, while opening myself to the meaning that's being transmitted from you to me.

Understanding another requires that I "tune in," almost as if the other person were a radio frequency. As I listen to you, I must search for ways to relate and empathize—ways to grasp the true meaning of your words and your actions. It is said that compassion is "*your* pain in *my* heart." To truly understand you, I've got to make room in my own head and heart and put myself in your shoes. In this way, listening is an act of compassion.

Unfortunately, most people never really learn to listen and empathize at this level. And that presents a serious problem.

Ninety-nine percent of the organizational consulting, team-building, and leadership coaching I do is a tutorial in how to really listen. Good listening is a cornerstone of organizational effectiveness, strong leadership, and exceptional customer service. The objective is to always leave the other person feeling respected and understood, and to make sure you leave on the same page. Sometimes our heads are so full of our own agendas and thoughts (i.e., "noise") at work that we're unable to really listen. We miss the boat completely. And our organizations suffer.

We've all developed lenses through which we see the world—some of them clear and some distorted. The clear ones tend to enable people to forge deep and lasting connections. To achieve great things and break through even the most stubborn impasses. The distorted ones can prevent us from understanding what others are really saying. They put us back on our heels, defending ourselves, leaving us unsatisfied. If we are going to live our best life, and be our most effective, we have to ask ourselves, "How good of a listener am I, really?" "How effective are my lenses in helping me understand and interact with others?"

I created a self-assessment tool in my coaching and consulting practice for businesses (couples and parents love it, too). It's called "The Listening Report Card." Listeners assess how effective they are by rating themselves from A–F in 25 different areas, from verbal responses to non-verbal communication, including body language. I then challenge them to take it a step further by doing one of two things. First, they can ask their co-workers (or spouses or kids) to grade them in these 25 areas. The areas include basic skills such as: knows when to remain silent, gives full attention, asks questions that show concern and caring, and exudes warmth and greets with a friendly, welcoming look. Second, they can conduct a video assessment of their approachability.

Getting Real—"The Listening Report Card"

This self-assessment tool measures how effective you are in listening. You can also compare your scores (A–F) in 25 key areas—with how those closest to you see you. Go to www.kendruck.com to find out more.

Most of us are unaware of the signals we give off, especially with our facial expressions. I sometimes use a video camera to assess the non-verbal "approachability" of my clients. We study the video to determine what "message" they might be sending through facial expressions and body language—and how they might be more effective listeners. A person's face and tone of voice might say: "Yeah, what?" "Go away, I don't have time for you," or "So good to see you. How can I be of help?"

Once each person has filled out their own Listening Report Card and has also asked to be graded by three or four people who know them well—people they either live with or interact with on a daily basis—we compare their responses. This affords the client a much fuller picture of his or her "actual" listening skills—and some great suggestions about how to improve.

It's remarkable how wide the discrepancies can be between people's self-assessment and that of their peers and family. Frankly, most of us have convinced ourselves that we're far better listeners than we really are. We also think that we are more approachable than we are in other people's eyes. Executives who pat themselves on the back for keeping the proverbial "open door" policy are often perplexed. "My door is open!" they say. "How come nobody is coming in?" Their door may be open, but their hearts, minds, and facial expressions are not. And this makes it risky or unsafe for others to enter. Parents and CEO's I coach are always delighted to discover the many simple, little things they can do to make themselves more approachable. Things like a warm smile, a personal greeting, showing appreciation, and remembering something personal that someone told you can go a long way.

The way we show another human being we care, the way we show them we respect and value them, is by really tuning in. Real Rule #8: Listening Is Love. Good listening is a key to every successful relationship, whether it's between a customer and salesman, boss and employee, parent and child, or husband and wife.

Being a Safe Haven

At the core of good listening is safety. Good listeners allow others a kind of safe haven—a place where they aren't judged, but where their thoughts and feelings are welcomed, respected, explored, and understood. The operative dynamics in every successful relationship are safety and inclusion. People have to feel safe being who they are and saying what they really feel. They have to feel understood and they have to be able to trust that you genuinely care. Ideally, you want all the people in your life to say, "Hey! I really count for something in his eyes. Nice."

One of my coaching clients, Carole, is a young executive who has quietly struggled with alcoholism for most of her young life. At age 38, Carole has been sober for a year, lost 30 pounds, and is in her first healthy adult relationship. While she's doing great, she has only developed *some* of the life skills required to sustain these positive changes. Despite all the good work she's done, when Carole came to see me she was feeling deeply discouraged and ready to give up.

"I can't do this!" she proclaimed. "I've never felt as bad as I'm feeling right now. This is just not working."

My response was to slow things down, really listen, and draw Carole out. After she had finished explaining why she felt this way and what had happened recently to cause her to feel this way, I commented, "I'm really sorry things are so hard for you right now Carole."

Our conversation began with me listening intently and, after she had gotten it all out, letting her know how badly I felt for her (validating her feelings and showing her I cared). I didn't take her by the shoulders and yell, "Pull it together! You've got a great life and a great new boyfriend, you're sober—why the hell are you so depressed? Stop whining, complaining, and feeling sorry for yourself! Shape up!" Instead, I invited her to tell me more about what was going on—and just listened.

Being able to confess how hard this all was, how inept she felt to face the world, how terrifying it was to be in a real relationship when she wasn't self-medicating, and how defenseless she felt against her old feelings of despair cleared the air. The judgment she had been using to beat herself up was gone. In its place was relief and self-acceptance.

Of course, she felt so very young (not in years, but in experience) and vulnerable. How understandable these feelings were, given the fact that Carole had not been "in class," figuratively speaking, since starting drugs and alcohol at age 15. Here she was, at age 38, struggling to cope with work and relationship challenges she had never before encountered. Of course, it all felt overwhelming.

But slowly, after she had gotten it all out, something shifted. We both sensed it. It had become okay for Carole to talk about how she was feeling; she felt safe doing so. Once she felt this sense of understanding and acceptance, she was able to make perfect sense of what she was feeling. These emotions weren't occurring in a vacuum. Her fear and despair came from having moved her life to a whole different level. It was new and scary and—most important—Carole could now see it was normal and understandable. She wasn't bad, or crazy. Just human!

As we kept talking, I could feel Carole beginning to perk up. It was like she was coming alive. Validating her feelings, and reframing them as "human," changed everything. I had served as the quiet hand on her shoulder, the calm voice of reassurance saying, "How understandable that you would be feeling that. How normal that you are afraid. How much sense it makes for you to feel scared and disheartened." I was acknowledging her humanity rather than putting a spin on her emotions or trying to fit them into some quick-fix scheme of self-reliance or "positive thinking."

At the end of our session, Carole confessed, "You know, I kind of expected you to tell me 'The glass if half full,' or make the excuse that I'm still so young! To give me some 'get back on the horse' response."

Those clichés are like putting a Band-Aid on a gunshot wound. Not only do they not help anything; they're insulting and dismissive. They also carry hidden messages. They seem to say, "It'll all be okay." But what they're really saying is, "I'm going to fix this (because I can't really handle what you're feeling and neither can you)." The real message is almost always hidden in the parentheses.

Honoring the way things were for her instead of trying to change the way she felt—reminding her we're all a work in progress—was all she needed to regain her footing. Listening alone validated the legitimacy of her struggle. Finally, there was somebody who really "got" it. She no longer felt so utterly alone in this world. I didn't pour sugar all over her experience or even sanction it. I simply validated that it was what it was for her.

I had the honor of meeting the Reverend Norman Vincent Peale, author of *The Power of Positive Thinking,* and his wife on several occasions. Reverend Peale would let those he was counseling speak at great length about their problems—without interrupting, putting a bow on things, giving them a hearty slap on the back and telling them to get over it, or informing them that "God is in charge" (something which makes a lot of people feel as if God is committing malpractice).

When the individual had finished venting his pain, Reverend Peale would just say the single word "But . . ." And then he would fall silent again, and invite the individual to consider, slowly at first and then with increasing enthusiasm, all the blessings in his life.

Good listening never has or needs spin. It's pure witnessing. It's about showing empathy and *being with* someone. All I did for my client was to try to put myself in her place. And as a result, this young woman felt deeply understood.

Listening in Love

The human experience of feeling understood is the basis for love and understanding. It's the way we reach out to those we care about, build trust, and connect. As theologian and philosopher Martin Buber noted, all real living is meeting. It's the meeting place of I and thou—the place where we connect that's neither you nor me. It's the place where we touch.

Truly listening to someone allows them to go deeper into their own heart and soul, their truth and longings. It's one of the most honorable things we can do in service to another person, precisely because it forms the very basis for knowing them. And knowing that person, heart to heart, soul to soul, allows us to truly love them.

This is why listening is so critical in the context of close relationships, and why the lack thereof can rip a couple or family or company apart.

A good buddy of mine recently had "The Talk" with his girlfriend after it had become clear that their once promising relationship was going sideways. Almost every conversation between them ended up in anger and defensiveness. Every time they tried, they hit nothing but dead ends. She was blaming him for the breakdown in communications between them. He was building a case for why it was all her fault. And their ship was slowly sinking.

I advised him to go for couples counseling.

A good couples' counselor or coach will slow each partner down and point out the places where there's little or no understanding because there's no real listening taking place. Without listening, there is no traction. Couples just spin their wheels and go nowhere fast.

Slowing down the process and reframing things in a more human light helps factor out the blame and defensiveness, and factor in the honesty, respect, truth, vulnerability, and caring which is often just underneath it. With an objective third party, it's no longer a contest between two people to see who's right. Each person, and the hurting relationship itself, are listened to and shown respect, as well as compassion.

There are few things as painful in a relationship as not feeling listened to or understood. Especially when you're talking to somebody you love. It can be despairing, disheartening, and discouraging. We suffer the same kind of "living loss" I talked about earlier. There really is something to the old saying that people don't care what you know until they know that you care. No strong and healthy relationship ever started by one person saying, "I really don't care about what you have to say." Loss of listening often leads to an erosion of confidence and trust in the other person.

The opposite is also true. New and wonderful relationships are forged every day because one person takes a moment to really listen to another. Maybe you're in the checkout line at the supermarket, and the person before you was rude and abrasive to the cashier. In a moment of kindness, you say to the cashier, "Having a rough day?" And then you genuinely listen to their response. What that says is, "I am sorry about what happened. And I care."

Getting Real—"Courageous Listening"

Courage is what it takes to stand up and speak; courage is also what it takes to sit down and listen. — Winston Churchill

Whether it's about a casual or long-term relationship with a person you love, or there's a business deal hanging in the balance, good listening can work wonders. One of my recently divorced buddies, Sean, has a prime example of this.

Sean had been locking horns with his teenage son. Unmotivated, bringing home bad grades, and showing absolutely no interest in school or having a social life, his son was growing more obstinate by the day. Sean was scared and frustrated, and showed it by criticizing and badgering his son. They experienced a total communication breakdown, with Sean playing the cop and his son feeling like a perpetual suspect.

When Sean requested some advice, I asked, "Would it work to sit down with your son and ask him what's really going on? Have things gotten so bad between you that this would not work?" He told me things had gotten considerably worse since he and his wife had split. "It must hurt like hell not to be able to have a simple conversation with your son," I commented. "What if you told him how sorry you are about the divorce and that you're concerned about how much it has affected him?" As tears began to roll down Sean's face, he opened up about how painful this past year had been for him and how much of a failure he felt like. We talked for a while and when he left, I could tell that he felt a lot lighter. And clearer.

The next call I got from Sean several months later was one of jubilation. He had checked his defensiveness at the door and decided to really find out how his son was doing, without trying to fix, change, modify, defend, or write himself into the script as "the savior." Instead of lecturing his son, he tried to just "be with" him as I had suggested.

And wouldn't you know it—everything began to change. They had a long talk and his son finally opened up. "Dad, I'm really having a hard time in school," he said. "I just don't care anymore. I'm always tired. Maybe I should get a checkup or something." That day, Sean scheduled a physical and they went to see what might be causing his exhaustion and lethargy. The doctor ruled out physical causes, diagnosed him with a mild depression, and referred him into counseling for kids going through divorce. It has made all the difference. Sean and his son are now side by side in each other's hearts instead of at each other's throats.

Sometimes, the decision to have a real conversation, to put all our cards on the table, is a decision to just listen.

Whether it's between a parent and child, among friends, within a family, or on an executive team where there's conflict, the willingness to sit down and have a real conversation—and to have it slowly, in a non-accusatory tone, can make all the difference. Good listening can help a struggling child, transform an entire company, revitalize a stagnant relationship, or save a marriage. Learning how to "be with" can truly change the course of your life.

Instructions to the Jury

The best philosophy for listening I've ever heard came from a completely unexpected place. I was in court, watching my nephew, who just so happens to be a deputy district attorney. As he completed his opening argument, the judge turned to the jury and gave them "instructions" for deliberating the guilt or innocence of the accused.

The instructions read: "It is important that you keep an open mind throughout this trial. Evidence can only be presented a piece at a time. Do not form or express an opinion about this case while the trial is going on. You must not decide on a verdict until after you have heard all the evidence and have discussed it thoroughly with your fellow jurors in your deliberations.

Getting Real—"Instructions to the Jury"

Suspending one's judgment and truly listening to the merits of what somebody is saying in an unbiased way, similar to the instructions a judge gives a jury, helps you truly tune in to the speaker.

"You must decide what the facts are in this case. And, I repeat, your verdict must be based only on the evidence that you hear or see in this courtroom. Do not let bias, sympathy, prejudice, or public opinion influence your verdict.

"You must follow the law as I explain it to you, even if you do not agree with the law."

Who knew that the civil courts could devise such brilliant advice for how to truly listen? And to show that you genuinely care!

I think the Instructions to the Jury, or some version of them, should be taught in communication classes, included in wedding vows, and read to every couple before marriage counseling. They should be read before a dad talks with his kids. Before an executive talks with their management team. Suspending one's judgment and truly listening to the merits of what somebody is saying in an unbiased way is a profound and powerful way of putting one's own emotions and reactions on hold and tuning in to the substance of any given conversation.

Now, it's not that you're not entitled to your own opinions and emotions. When people say stuff, you're going to want to react. That's natural. But what is required for good listening is to temporarily put your own feelings and opinions aside in service to the other person. Right now, if I'm listening to you, it's about you. It's not about what I feel, what I may think, or whether I agree. It's not about my personal reaction. All of that can come later—after I have a true understanding of your position. And, if I've done a good job demonstrating I care about you by listening well, then you're more likely to want to listen to me in return.

Executive coaching shows a client how to maximize every conversation by being an exceptional listener. At the beginning of a conversation, I suggest both parties make a statement of good intention. "What I want from bringing this issue up is . . ." That conveys good faith. I call this technique "prefacing."

Prefacing means, quite literally, setting a clear and positive tone for the conversation that's about to take place. In a corporate environment, you might say, "The reason I wanted to talk with you is to _____. I'd like to talk for a few minutes, without interruption or comment. Then, I'd love to hear your thoughts and brainstorm about how to move forward. I'm hoping we can come out of this with _____ [the desired outcome]."

Getting Real—"Prefacing"

Prefacing is simply setting the tone for a conversation; it lets the other parties know what you want to discuss, your good intentions, and a desired outcome.

This can be immensely helpful in sensitive, emotionally-charged conversations where the potential for greater clarity, trust, and understanding is needed to bring about change. Whether it's your partner or sibling or best friend, giving the other person 10 to 15 minutes to state their case, explain their intention, and articulate their desired outcome sets the table for communication and relationship breakthroughs.

Prefacing is important because most of the time, we go into conversations blindly. We *assume* what the other person, or the group, wants and expects. Then, afterward, we wonder, "Isn't that what you wanted? Isn't that why you brought this up?" We don't realize that people bring things up for a variety of reasons. And sometimes—perhaps even most of the time—they just want to know that somebody cares enough to really listen. When two people are really listening to one another, the possibilities for making new agreements, healing old wounds, getting through impasses, and creating a positive future together are unlimited.

True listening doesn't mean, "All right, yeah, okay, got it, thanks" or "Yes, but . . ." These phrases smack of impatience. I'm talking about listening that's *real* and *authentic*. Selfless. Uncontaminated. Patient. Compassionate. Free of projection or unsolicited advice. It's about you, the other person, and your mutual well-being. Good listening is time and attention given freely and unbegrudgingly, in service to understanding the other person—and whatever's on their mind. This listening has no agenda other than to care and learn. There is no fixing, no analysis or opinion. It is the simplest and purest expression of a meeting between two souls.

As Kahlil Gibran writes in *The Prophet*, "And when he is silent your heart ceases not to listen to his heart." Even when there is silence, we possess the breathtaking capacity to really listen from heart to heart.

Real Action

RR#8 TAKEAWAYS

EXERCISE #1 Becoming a more effective listener requires tuning in and mastering the art of asking open-ended or clarifying questions. Check the questions that you would agree to start asking more frequently.

❏ "I am not sure what you mean. Could you please explain?"

❏ "What was it like for you when that happened?"

❏ "What do you think your next step should be?"

❏ "What are your options?"

❏ "Can you tell me more?"

❏ "When you say [insert what the person has said], what I'm hearing is that [insert your interpretation of what was said]. Is that correct?"

EXERCISE #2 Take the Listening Report Card on my website, www.kendruck.com, and list five of your best strengths and biggest limitations.

EXERCISE #3 Write down three things that are getting in the way of you becoming a better listener (as a leader, teammate, parent, or friend/confidant).

EXERCISE #4 List five things you can do to make yourself more approachable.

EXERCISE #5 Name three people you feel best understand you. Next to each person write down what you do to help bring this about.

EXERCISE #6 Name one person who you wish would listen to you better.

Real Rule #9

CLOSURE IS A MYTH:
Healing Is a Lifelong Process

Closure. Anyone who's ever experienced loss has heard about it, prayed for it, wanted it desperately. Whether someone close to you has died or you've suffered devastating financial losses, you've invariably heard that closure is what you're supposed to be seeking, and what, at some point, you're sure to attain.

In theory, it's a great concept. Who wouldn't want to be "finished" and done with the pain of loss? It's human nature to want to tie everything up in a neat little bow—to get "over" the parts of life that hurt. Some of us even approach loss with a checklist in hand. "Anger? Check! Sorrow? Check! Okay, now can I get on with my life?"

If only life (and getting over a loss) were that easy.

Imagine if I said to my friend whose daughter had been murdered, "Just do A, B, and C, and you'll get over it." So he sees a grief counselor, goes to a support group, starts taking an antidepressant, and goes for daily coffee with a buddy (in that order). He's going down the checklist.

A year later, his daughter's murderer is convicted. The man comes back to me and says, "I did everything you said—I checked all the boxes off. And now the guy's been put away. But all that stuff is coming up again. I thought when the trial ended, that would be it. Everyone said, 'At least you have closure now.' But there's no relief. In fact, I feel worse. So what is wrong with me? I told myself a lie about what would happen when this trial ended . . . and you let me do it."

I never give people an "ABC" checklist because grief doesn't work that way. There's no rhyme or reason to the healing process after a loss. Many years ago, my friend and mentor, Elisabeth Kübler-Ross, a true pioneer of the hospice movement, wrote about what has come to be widely accepted as the "stages" of grief. And yet, near the end of her life, when we would meet at her home, Elisabeth would tell me her stages were meant to be guideposts, not a cookie-cutter prescription for getting closure. Trying to sanitize our feelings, tie them up in a neat little package, and expect we're all going to go through a series of orderly stages is only setting ourselves up for more pain.

Grief has a life and a timetable all its own. Each of us comes to terms with loss in our own time and our own way. In my experience, there is no such thing as real closure. Yes, certain events can be finished. Maybe the trial or the funeral are over, or you finally got the court papers finalizing your divorce. A painful chapter comes to a welcome end. But that doesn't mean all the feelings associated with these events are suddenly going to cease and desist. Why do we feel that it's necessary to put a period at the end of a sentence when we don't know what the future holds?

It's natural that we want to make things final—to be done with painful and unpleasant parts of our lives and move on. These losses are such a source of pain, humiliation, frustration, distress, and disturbance in our lives. But we can't always block our hearts or minds, nor should we try. Some things just hurt for a long time, not because of any fault or failure on our part—despite what we're often led to believe. Some feelings are just going to be there for the rest of our lives. As baseball legend/cult philosopher Yogi Berra so wisely said, "It ain't over till it's over."

If you're beating yourself up for not finding closure, take it easy and back off. There's nothing wrong with you. You can't find something that doesn't exist.

Some Things Occur Outside of Time

In my line of work, there's a lot of speculation about the length and stages of the healing process. Some want to know, "How long is this going to take?" In alcohol recovery people ask, "How long before I can start drinking again?" In the initial stages of grief, it is not uncommon for a newly bereaved Mom or Dad to ask, "How long is this going to go on? I'm not sure how much longer I can take it. What are the steps I need to follow?"

Often there's a made-up recovery period or deadline attached to a crisis or transition we're going through. "Divorce? Oh, should take about a year." "Lost job? Should be okay in six months." A bereaved wife recently told me, "My new psychologist told me it should take one year to get over the death of my husband. It's been over a year. What am I doing wrong?" she asked.

It's a complaint I hear often, "What's wrong with me?" Or, "I did everything everybody told me and I'm still missing my Dad." Years after a loss, people are still missing their loved ones. How could they not? Those who lost loved ones with violent suddenness struggle with the painful memories, intrusive thoughts, and unwelcome flashbacks so common to traumatic loss. They're convinced they must be doing something wrong or these things wouldn't be happening.

I encourage these people to forget about all the old wives' tales and clichés, to let themselves off the hook and allow themselves to be human. Not that they should allow grief and loss to take control of their lives. They just need to be honest with themselves and others about how they're really doing, so they can get the support they need. In the ruthless quest for closure and approval, we end up dehumanizing and hurting ourselves. We're expecting something that is unreasonable if not impossible, which is to know in advance when we'll be over our loss. Yes, a chapter may be closed. And progress should be noted, even celebrated. But there are often new chapters yet to be written, and there's no way to determine when or what they will be.

Take the example of my client whose daughter was murdered. At the time, he had been married to the same woman for 24 years. Within three years of his daughter's death, they were divorced. That happened more than a decade ago. At the time, all he could deal with was his daughter's death. But only in the last couple of years did he actually start grieving the death of his marriage. Only recently did he realize how angry he had been with his ex-wife. How betrayed he felt by her leaving. His grief over the loss of his daughter had eclipsed everything else for so long, and only after ten years was he able to truly deal with issues arising from the end of his marriage. He had no way of knowing this "chapter" would resurface so many years down the line. How could he? So much for closure!

Should people who have prematurely declared "closure" push away these kinds of feelings when they come up? Should they fake it to appear normal again, while inwardly feeling like they are doing something wrong? That they are failures?

Absolutely not! The second part of Real Rule #9 is that healing is a *lifelong process*. Old pain often recycles when triggered. Unfinished business comes up again, bubbling to the surface long after we think it "should" be gone. And it arises for reasons that are not always clear. Maybe we're finally ready for it. Maybe it was too emotionally overwhelming at the time it happened for us to deal with it all at once, and now we have the strength to process even more. Like a shard of shrapnel that's been stuck beneath our skin—sitting there for years and never surfacing—until finally, one day, our bodies expel them. Perhaps it's the same with our minds and hearts. Old wounds surface when it's time! As part of the natural healing process, when we are ready.

Getting Real—"Lifelong Healing"

Healing may be a lifelong process, but we do have some say in the way the process unfolds. If we block off our emotions and refuse to acknowledge the way we are feeling over time, it stymies our natural ability to grow, heal, learn, move past the tragedy, and write new chapters of life.

In my Grief Literacy and Healing After Loss workshops, I like to point out that we have a choice. We get to express how we feel—or we get to stuff it. "Processed" grief has been allowed to work its way through our system and express itself in some constructive way. "Unprocessed" grief is stuff that we're not dealing with, which will express itself too—it's just likely to come out "sideways." Unprocessed grief has a tendency to turn into numbness, aggression, and indifference to the pain of others.

Look at all the incarcerated kids in the California Youth Authority (CYA)—hundreds of thousands of kids under 21 who are in jail. One study showed that most of these kids first started getting into trouble after they'd incurred a significant life loss. Might it be possible that the adults in their lives glossed over the fact that they lost someone or something very important to them, and that these kids were hurting terribly?

Too many of our disenfranchised children, rich and poor, get the message to "suck it up" and "get over it and move on." They feel that nobody really cares about their pain. So what do they do? They spread that pain around. Their anger or indifference to the pain of others shows up glaringly in juvenile crime (drug, homicide, and suicide) statistics.

If they were given time to process their loss—with a significant adult who cares and supports them—I guarantee we'd see a lot fewer gang members and violent offenders at the CYA. Not to mention less violence on the streets, a lot fewer suicides, and fewer kids strung out on drugs.

Closure as Comfort Food

If closure is a myth, then why do people always ask—after every breakup, death, and loss—if we feel we've "gotten closure" and can finally move on with our lives?

Because closure is comfort food. It gives us temporary relief from the pain. The idea of closure—the belief that there is a light at the end of the tunnel—makes us comfortable. It theoretically gives us a way to fill the emptiness we feel with hope. Hope that the pain will soon be over. We want to paint a pretty face on the loss. And when someone close to us suffers a loss is it any surprise that we don't really know how to be there for them? Witnessing someone else's loss activates all of our worst fears—the "what if" scenarios that we spend a lot of energy, time, and resources running away from because they leave us feeling so weak and powerless.

Because it's an unfeasible ideal, our insistence that people get closure can turn into something hurtful. It's like we're sapping the natural emotions out of an individual who's suffered a loss and pumping some artificial chemical back into his or her system. In other words: we're embalming the living with false hope.

Messages like "Get back out there!" don't help. Sometimes even close friends and family members jump on the bandwagon, suggesting we "Get back on the horse!" before we're ready. The underlying message is: "You are making all of us feel very uncomfortable. Can't you just move on?"

The presence of pain and anguish, and the anxiety of not knowing how to help, often cause well-meaning people to gloss over and put a spin on the distress of others. When confronted with the helplessness of someone who's in pain, we defer to our knee-jerk reaction: the "figure out and fix" two-step.

Oh, But You're So Young!

After 9/11, The Jenna Druck Center started a variety of grief support groups in New York. One of them was for young widows of the 343 firefighters who lost their lives at Ground Zero. These women ran the gamut from 18- and 19-year-old newlyweds to 30-somethings with kids. When I asked them, "Tell me one thing people say that helps you and one that makes you want to throw them to the ground and choke them," the answers were pretty universal.

"What's most helpful is when people simply say how sorry they are," the young women all agreed. "What drives us most crazy is when they say, 'Oh, but you're so young!'"

What does "But you're so young!" actually mean? The underlying message being delivered to those women was, "Don't be so sad! You'll have no problem finding a substitute husband." It's similar to the seemingly innocent question bereaved parents get all the time: "Do you have any other children?" There's this underlying message of, "Look, get over it already. You've got another one!"

Let me be the first to tell you, every one of those widows and parents wanted to scream, "It's not all right! I am sad! And there's nothing you can say or do to make it better! It just sucks!"

It doesn't matter if you've lost your home, health, pension, life-savings, marriage, or business—or a loved one to cancer or terrorism—messages like these make you feel utterly alone, misunderstood, and judged. Suddenly you're dealing with a second loss: the abandonment of society. These "get over it" messages are blatantly insensitive, as are the many other things people say to help, even the family members who love you. But they don't help. They hurt. And sometimes, though we don't even know it, we "join in" and do it to ourselves.

Getting Real—"Don't Get Over It"

"Get over it" messages shut us down. Told to just get over it and move on, it's easy to understand why we would want to turn away from, and even deny, our pain, shaming and blaming ourselves.

That insidious voice of self-criticism eats away at us from the inside out. "What's wrong with me?" we want to know. We can all be unrelenting in our judgment of ourselves. The voice of self-condemnation in those who have suffered deep wounds, like rape victims and disabled veterans, can be brutal.

My scars are ugly! they think. *Look at me! I'm damaged merchandise!* The antidote for such harsh self-judgment is the voice of self-compassion and kindness. Self-compassion starts not from a position of what's *wrong* with you, but from a position of what's *right*. How could you suffer great loss, trauma, or pain and not feel the way you feel? How could you *not* be going through what you're going through? And how could you *not* feel the effects of such an ordeal? Self-compassion says, "Rest assured:

you're doing the very best you can. And with greater kindness and compassion for yourself, you'll do even better tomorrow."

This voice of gentle self-acceptance is one that most of us could use more often, especially when we're hurting. It takes great effort and determination to break the grip of old insidious habits when it comes to a critical and condemning voice. Learning to speak in a kind and encouraging voice gives us the strength, support, and permission we need to get to the next step in a long healing process. What's more, once we stop shaming ourselves our physical and emotional wounds and scars can even become badges of honor and reminders of our bravery.

Forward Movement

At the Jenna Druck Center, we have a saying about the pain of suffering a loss: "It never gets better. It gets different."

Most people don't want to hear that. It's one of the Real Rules that many people do not want to accept. But accepting the fact that some wounds heal very slowly and unevenly and that some things never get better can be one of the most freeing things you can do for yourself. By putting to rest the idea that it should "get better," you can stop berating yourself for not feeling better or "getting closure." Instead, you can open to all there is to be grateful for: the people and blessings that are helping you move forward in your life.

Though in our darkest moments it seems impossible, we do truly make forward movement. Moment by moment, we begin putting one foot in front of the other. This slow and steady movement brings newfound energy and strength to deal with feelings that show up months and years after the initial loss. These feelings don't resurface to harass, punish, or torment you; they resurface to show you that you still have some processing to do. And that's not only okay; it's often just the roadmap you need for continued healing.

Unfinished, unprocessed parts of our lives will float back up the top, often in dreams and memories. One day you'll be inexplicably angry; another day surprisingly lighthearted; another day a feeling of sorrow will pass over you like a shadow. All of these experiences are totally normal, and provide subtle reminders to go easy on yourself. You are a work in progress and still have healing to do.

It might take ten years for shrapnel to surface through the skin. Or it could be 20. There are no timelines, no conditions. It will take what it will take. And we can go on with life in the meantime. As healing and reconciliation unfold in each of our lives, we acknowledge and validate the feelings that surface. Honest acknowledgment encourages forward movement.

In the end, we do not need closure to heal. Nor do we need it to "get better." As the family members with whom I was reunited at the ten-year anniversary of 9/11 reaffirmed, it is courage, patience, and small steps forward, one breath at a time, that carve the path for vibrant new chapters to be written.

Real Action

RR#9 TAKEAWAYS

Closure is a myth, but healing isn't. There's much relief to be found in that simple acknowledgment.

EXERCISE #1 How might you allow a healing process to unfold in your life?

- Change my "message to myself" from 90 percent self-criticism to 90 percent self-compassion.

- Stop telling myself (and allowing others to tell me) to "Get over it!" and instead, face the real feelings that are there.

EXERCISE #2 List five ways you have made forward movement in your life after a setback.

EXERCISE #3 List several events or experiences from the past that you still beat yourself up for. Next to each one complete the sentence that begins "I could stop beating myself up for this if I only . . . ."

EXERCISE #4 With a confidant, explore the terms and conditions under which you would be willing to forgive yourself. If you're the kind of person that really has it in for yourself, consider getting professional help to reverse this self-destructive pattern.

Real Rule #10

CONTROL IS AN ILLUSION:
Knowing When
It's Time to Let Go

Human beings are interesting creatures. We think we rule the world, but at the same time, we're all aliens.

As newborns, we're plopped down on this strange planet without the faintest clue of how to maneuver it. So we start from scratch as we attempt to figure it all out—how to walk, how to talk. We try desperately to make some semblance of order and meaning out of utter chaos. Is it any wonder that we scream bloody murder when we're born? And that we go through "the terrible two's" a few years later?

My daughter, Stefie, used to scream out of frustration as an infant. At first, I tried everything to get her to stop. But "shushing" her did not work. In time, like most parents, I learned her different cries. Most of the time it wasn't hunger or a dirty diaper—she was just feeling over-whelmed by the experience of being a new human. Recognizing this, I did my best to comfort, and even encourage, her. I'd say, "You go ahead and get it out, sweetheart. It's okay." Crying out in frustration, confusion, and humiliation is normal and healthy. Stefie would get out all her feelings and then she'd be fine. Now a young woman, she'll say,

"Looking back, my Dad was not your typical father. Raising a parent is not easy."

Nor is it easy for kids to grow up. We learn how to fold our hands nicely in our laps and sit up straight at our desks. We learn to domesticate those wild, untamed parts of ourselves; to still all that confusion and chaos. To control our impulses and emotions through silence, repression, and lots of "shushing."

It's in our nature to want to be in control of our own lives. No one likes uncertainty, and we all want to look good in our endeavor to master our time here on earth. "Look at my name in the credits!" we want to say during the course of our lives, and even on our deathbed. "That's me! Writer, director, producer, choreographer—I did it all!"

And it almost works. Sometimes we succeed at controlling the outcome of our lives—at least in certain situations. The control freaks among us become very skilled at choreographing certain aspects of our existences, which makes us feel safe and powerful. We develop great internal resources (creativity, tenacity, etc.) and external networks (relationships, businesses) to make things go our way. And for a while—maybe even years—it seems like we're in complete control.

But at some point, each of us learns that we can't control everything all the time. The times we succeeded were often only because "the forces that be" in the universe were cooperating with our agendas. But life is such that at some point, they won't. The stars won't be aligned in our favor, and we will have setbacks. Chances are you already have.

We're not the only ones holding the reins of our lives, and never have been. As we said earlier, life is going to have its say.

So, how do we respond when it does?

Getting older and doing life-expectancy math in our heads, we begin to understand just how vulnerable we are. Our mortality, spirituality, and a sense of urgency compel us to make peace with life and death. (Exactly how we go about this is the subject of my Courageous Aging workshops.)

Out of Our Hands

Unexpected changes in our lives are the hardest wake-up call of all. We realize that control is an illusion. The more we cling to that illusion, the more difficulty we will experience in finding any semblance of peace. It's a vicious cycle: because we're trying to avoid loss, we end up holding on ever tighter. When we're hurt, frightened, and trying to control everything, we are more prone to losing what we love.

This is extremely problematic when it comes to relationships. The more we try to control another person, the harder it is to get close to them. As a matter of fact, the attempt to control another person puts us at greater risk of losing them. Nobody wants to be suffocated and told what to do. Even if they *do* stay, you may lose them emotionally.

"Since we sold the house and moved into a condo," a client of mine named Jill explained, "I can't get Bill off my back for five minutes. He's a nervous wreck and it's getting to me. I don't want to be around him anymore so I leave for work early and go to bed early." Even the most devoted partners like Jill can become frustrated, discouraged, and even resentful of an overbearing spouse that they distance themselves.

This can be one of the most devastating kinds of losses. We feel our partner drifting further and further away, and a sense of failure and loneliness overtakes us even as we are still in the relationship. The idea that our partner is sleeping a foot away from us and yet they feel totally untouchable, unreachable, and unapproachable can be excruciatingly painful. For many this is the worst kind of aloneness—when the distance between two people is vast, and they feel helpless to close the gap.

We essentially have two choices: to hold life's unknowns in gentle hands—hoping, praying, working hard for them to get better, and allowing them to unfold—or we can clench them with a closed, tight fist, fearing the worst, trying frantically to control everything and driving ourselves and everyone around us crazy in the process. Those of us who hold on tightly might be better off learning to loosen our grip a little.

Getting Real—"True Serenity" and Peace

The root of "serenity" is the Latin word **serenus,** which means clear, cloudless, and untroubled. When you loosen your hold on life's unknowns, your state of mind becomes like a perfectly clear blue sky without a cloud in it.

You've probably heard the Serenity Prayer, penned by the American theologian and philosopher Reinhold Niebuhr. "God, grant me the serenity to accept the things I cannot change; the courage to change the things I can; and the wisdom to know the difference." This simple prayer, a hallmark of Alcoholics Anonymous, is now widely known to the general population because it rings so true for all of us.

Compulsive over-control isn't just the alcoholic, workaholic, or shopaholic's burden to bear. It's a characteristic of anyone who is afraid. Anyone who has been hitting their head against the wall and is now trying to recalibrate their expectations about just how much control is possible in life. If the world feels out of control, a fearful person tries to control the people around them. Thus we all become entangled in power struggles and endless dramas.

Ironically, instead of tightening our hold, we have to learn how to loosen our grip. Let go a little instead of holding on so tightly. This is true whether you're dealing with your romantic partner, your kids, your company, your aging, or your mortality. Practice on the smaller things— like letting go of your kids when you send them to their first day of kindergarten or off to college. Our children are the best reminders of Real Rule #10—it's never as obvious that control is an illusion as when we're dealing with our kids!

What We Can Control

There's a lot we can do to best insure the safety and well-being of our family, ourselves, and the freedoms we cherish. Sometimes this may involve taking charge and kicking ass, so we need to be prepared to do exactly that. But it may also mean sharing, or even surrendering, control. Ultimately, life is not something we can control completely. We may squeeze down until our knuckles are white, but it doesn't matter. Some things remain out of our hands.

When we simply acknowledge that we are living life partly on life's terms, it is no longer necessary to control everything. Relinquishing the illusion of control is one of the greatest gifts we can give ourselves and those around us. It also opens us to one of life's biggest mysteries, which is that only when we let go of expectations can the wonderfully unexpected appear. Only when we empty our minds can we experience a life-changing revelation. Only when we allow ourselves to experience our separateness do we discover how much a part of everything we really are.

We're all "a work in progress." There's no completed masterpiece among human beings. But the more honest we are in dealing with our fears, and the less we play them out on the stage of life, the less need we feel to control others and their responses. And the more peaceful and free we become as a result.

Might this be a good time to let someone else take the steering wheel once in a while? To learn to let go and trust?

✦ ✦ ✦

Real Action

RR#10 TAKEAWAYS

Control is an illusion; the more tightly we hold onto it, the more it slips through our fingers.

EXERCISE #1 Put a check mark next to the beliefs and behaviors that might be help you achieve more serenity and peace.

❏ Let go of trying to control others. Let them be who they will be.

❏ Let go of trying to control everything in your life. Let some things come to you.

❏ Loosen your grip on your children. If they don't fall down and learn to pick themselves up, they'll never grow.

❏ Give yourself permission to heal over the full course of your lifetime, if that's what it takes.

EXERCISE #2 Might you inadvertently be sending quick-fix "get over it" messages to anyone in your life? If so, write down whom. Next to their name, write down what you could do or say to be more sensitive, understanding, and empathetic. Then do it!

EXERCISE #3 Some of us don't think we're being overly self-critical—and we are. Some of us think we're being self-compassionate—and we're not. Which one do you suspect may be true of you? What makes you suspect this?

EXERCISE #4 List three things could you do to edit your inner voice so it is kinder and more understanding.

Real Rule #11

JOY IS A MUSCLE:
Putting More Joy into
Your Everyday Life

Sometimes the greatest challenge in life is not the hardship or suf-fering. It's the joy.

So often we have more difficulty experiencing the joy and miracles life has to offer than surviving the sorrow and suffering. As author Mari-anne Williamson says in her famous quote, "Our deepest fear is not that we are inadequate. Our deepest fear is that we are powerful beyond mea-sure. It is our light, not our darkness, that most frightens us."

In the 1980s, I heard about a wonderful workshop called The Joy of Singing and gave it to my wife as a birthday present. She had a beautiful voice that she rarely used. What better gift than to unleash the joy she already possessed. The genius behind this groundbreaking workshop was a former Broadway actor named Warren Lyons. Citing his own fears and self-criticism as inhibitors of joy and spontaneity, Warren coached workshop participants of every age and background to vanquish the "wagging finger of self-condemnation" and sing their hearts out. After a week of learning to rise above stubborn self-criticism and fear, they all did, including my wife, at a live concert for family members and friends.

With the exception of our children's births, I can never recall my wife as having been so joyful and happy.

Many of us have within our reach the joy of singing, dancing, painting, acting, writing, and other wonderful forms of creative expression. And yet we hold back. It can take time to free ourselves of the shame, fear, embarrassment, and self-criticism that keep us from joy. This is especially true for those of us who have depended on alcohol, drugs, food, and work to feel good. But we're worth it! Workshops, classes, therapies, and other programs that specialize in teaching people to uninhibit and express themselves, to gain confidence and experience the joy of just being alive, are often a great place to start.

Another reason we miss out on our greatest birthright as human beings—that is, to live lives rich with joy and purpose—is simple: our mismanagement of energy and time. In today's fast-paced world, too few of us are inclined to make time to rejoice and celebrate and savor the blessings that already exist in our lives.

We hear it so much that it's become clichéd. "Live in the moment!" bumper stickers cry. "Live in the now!" self-help books declare. Movies like *The Bucket List* preach the importance of living life in all its fullness before your time on earth is up. Embracing each day of your life as a cherished gift, and each person you love as precious. And yet, no matter how easy it is to talk about counting our blessings, cherishing our families, and living in the light, it still seems to be one of the most difficult things to do.

All we get is this moment. If we don't learn to live in this fleeting, eternal moment, then we experience the ultimate loss: the living of our lives.

But "being in the now" is easier said than done, right? A lot of us remain mired in the past and fixated on the future. We fail to open our eyes, ears, senses, and hearts to what's happening right here, right now. The intimacy of a relationship we're in. The beauty of nature around us. The prosperity we enjoy. Or, on the other hand, we're wired to go go go; there's just no PAUSE or STOP buttons built into our software. We are "runners," moving in ten different directions at once. We're escape artists, slipping away almost invisibly from the here and now. As a result, we blow right past life's most precious moments and miss the best parts of the ride!

Until we overcome our addiction to nonstop activity and diversion, and until we figure out how to pause, experience, and savor the moment—rather than running and escaping—we're never going to receive life's richness. We're never going to be satisfied. We're never going to feel a sense of gratitude or peace. We'll just keep rushing on to the next thing—the next "fix" of activity—and justifying it as necessary.

Real Rule #11 says: Joy Is a Muscle. If you don't learn to flex it, the best parts of your life are going to pass you by. And this is not just a cliché! It's a reality!

Slow It All Down

One of the best metaphors for Real Rule #11 is, unsurprisingly, sex.

There's a stark difference between hurried, outcome-oriented sex and truly making love with your partner. Everybody loves a good orgasm. But reaching a climax is a part of the ride and not the ride itself. Enjoying the process of fully loving another human being is the best part of the ride—and leads to infinitely greater satisfaction (and, often, orgasms).

I have a 90-year-old buddy who talks unabashedly about the exhilarating sweetness of holding and caressing his 89-year-old wife. At their age, there's no more acrobatic sex. But the tenderness and affection they share is so completely satisfying, they don't need anything more.

Relationships afford infinite potential to be deeply satisfied in ways that might surprise us. And that includes both sexual and non-sexual intimacy. There are endless possibilities for showing your love, affection, and desire to another person—ways that don't involve sex.

Of course, try telling that to the Viagra generation. It's a pervasive cultural message to men: everything good comes from an erection. But in its absence, new ways to "connect" present themselves. There are actually increased opportunities for pleasure, romance, satisfaction, and fulfillment, and for achieving a deep sense of connectedness with the person you love.

Do you see the analogy? It isn't just about sex—it's about our propensity as a society to focus only on the outcome. It's all about winning the prize, crossing the finish line, closing the deal. And everything that led up to it is secondary.

Getting Real—"Tantra"

Tantra was born in India more than 6,000 years ago as a way to rebel against the acetic status quo. Those who practice Tantra believe that sex actually expands consciousness—it's meant "to manifest, to expand, to show and to weave." Tantra expands mere moments of sexual ecstasy into a lifetime of sexual bliss. As a metaphor, it's about savoring every moment of a lifelong ride.

The Way We Really Win

We've all heard the expression, "It's about the journey, not the destination"—meaning the true joy in life comes from the process of getting to where you want to be. I'd like to take this adage a step further. Not only is the journey where we find true joy, but it's where we find true victory. Unlike what our overly competitive society tells us, the one who enjoys the race is even more of a winner than the one who crosses the finish line.

Olympic skier Bode Miller has gotten a lot of flak for demonstrating this attitude. For Miller, it isn't all about the win—though he's certainly racked up plenty of medals. In interviews from Vancouver 2010, he talked a lot about doing the best he could and being happy with his performance. Sure, he wanted to win gold, but that wasn't his only goal. And this is from the guy who's considered to be the greatest American alpine skier of all time!

The media jumped all over Miller in the last Olympics because of his laid-back attitude. He was criticized for his apparent lack of competitiveness—his "come what may" attitude. Poor Bode was just trying to enjoy the ride! How dare he, when "winning" is sitting atop the medal board? Shame on him!

The same thing happens in professional football. We get so locked into getting the result we want that we miss everything else. The New Orleans Saints win the Super Bowl in 2010, and Colts' quarterback Peyton Manning is sitting in the locker room in utter despair. He's so destroyed that he doesn't want to talk to anyone. It's as if all his success up to that point—how brilliantly the Colts played the whole season—was negated. Because if you come in second, you might as well have come in last. Or as famed coach Vince Lombardi put it, "Winning isn't everything, it's the only thing."

How many of us suffer the same self-imposed feelings of failure? We never become president of the company. We write ten books but none of them ever hits the jackpot. If we have kids, we aren't paraded out in front of the PTA as Mother or Father of the Year. So we feel like we failed; like we weren't good enough to really "make" it.

But what about all the joy and triumph and pride that sits dormant, like a million-dollar check that's never been cashed? The acclaim you deny and deflect? How about all the praise you are entitled to for being an excellent employee, a brilliant writer, a loving wife, a wonderful parent? It doesn't matter if you never got any plaques or trophies. Validation, adoration, and glory are cool, don't get me wrong. (I still have a trophy I got in high school.) We all need an occasional "'attaboy." But counting on somebody else to tell us that we have been a good parent, employee, or spouse, or that we're "winners," is too often a setup for disappointment. So how do we really become (and go out) winners? How do we cash that check?

Getting Real—"The Risks of Type-A"

Being goal-oriented is fine; just be wary of type-A behavior, which is linked to higher incidents of coronary heart disease, high cholesterol, chronic irritability, and free-floating anger.

Learning to Bless and Approve

By stopping and acknowledging our own value and achievements, we learn how to bless our lives. And not just at the end, but over the course of them. Unconditionally. For better or worse. We did the very best we could at the time. And we did well! Instead of waiting for a stamp of approval from the world, we can approve of ourselves.

Changing some of our criteria for what constitutes a real victory or success is not always easy. Learning to give credit and approval to ourselves is not always a simple matter. Changing the scoring system takes time and practice, but it's well worth the effort. And in the end, it's the only way to come out a real winner.

Stop and Smell the Roses . . . Literally

A few years ago, I was giving a team-building workshop for a Fortune 500 company. After the morning meetings, I took the CEO aside and spoke with him. He had been so tense and driven all morning, he was unable to relax and see "the bigger picture." Focused on everything that had gone wrong, or might go wrong, he was missing all the things that were going right. This was obvious to everyone but him. It was seriously affecting his ability to lead his company through a rough spot. "Walk outside to the courtyard," I instructed him. "Go to the rose bushes and literally smell them."

Twenty minutes later, he came back in and said, "All right, I smelled the roses—all one hundred and fifty-four of them. Now what?"

What a perfect illustration for how we live our lives today. Even smelling the roses becomes just another task to finish so we can get to the next thing!

His inability to drop into a deeper emotion, thought, or self-reflection—to keep everything that was happening around him in perspective—was becoming problematic for his team. He had become so desensitized that their effort seemed unimportant and incidental to him. The only thing that mattered was results ("the numbers"). Missing was any semblance of gratitude or appreciation. Performing the work had itself become an obstacle—a source of annoyance on his way to the big prize. He blew right past a garden of 154 beautiful, fragrant roses—not to mention his beautiful home, a family that loved him, and good health. He was doing the same with the loyal, hardworking members of his leadership team.

If we listen to the Real Rules, we realize that life itself is the prize. The process of living/working and treating others well are the real currency. Learning to draw deep satisfaction from the glorious experience of being the best we can be, day after day; loving the people we love in the best way we know how; and living our "small" life is, ironically, the biggest win.

Life is the gift that we've been given. It comes with countless blessings, large and small. All we have to do is aspire to be the very best we can. And there are so many levels of satisfaction that have nothing to do with winning the Super Bowl or earning the gold medal—things that truly constitute a good life, a noble effort, a job well done, a kind word, and heroic service.

The real wins in our lives are more often the small, subtle things that go unnoticed. The simple act of staying up late at night with a child who is sick or needs help with their homework. A thoughtful text message in the middle of the day from a husband or wife saying, "My life gets better each day with you in it." A heartfelt condolence card from your boss with a $250 check inside to "help with funeral expenses." Those barely noticeable acts of kindness and love can constitute greatness as much as any championship ever could.

What constitutes greatness in your life? What acts of kindness color your day? How can you make a subtle but significant difference in your world? Have you allowed other people, or society, to define success, failure, and significance for you? You can make significant contributions all the time. You can be proud of how you lived, how you conducted yourself as a son, daughter, husband, wife, parent, or the leader of a company. It's up to you to change the yardstick!

Balancing the process and the product can be a challenge. While it's perfectly okay for us to have goals and aspire to achieve them, to hold ourselves to high standards and exceptional results, we must also make it a goal to maintain the enjoyment of the ride—the attitude of gratitude—and the daily counting of our blessings.

So in a minute I am going to ask you to answer a few questions. What would have to happen for you to be more joyful? More grateful? What would have to change in you for you to enjoy this crazy, unpredictable ride known as life? And to savor what is already good? What specific "enjoyment muscles" have atrophied that, if exercised, would permit you to feel greater freedom, satisfaction, openness, trust, and joy (without having to win the lottery)?

The time to pull joy off of the sidelines and get it back in the game is now! Real Rule #11: Joy Is a Muscle. It needs to be exercised to stay vital and vibrant. Getting to experience life's many triumphs, blessings, and goodness is to savor them, relish them, generate them, and live in the gratitude of them. And so, when you come upon an opportunity to really let go, kick up your heels, and dance to the tune of your own song, don't hold back! Go for it!

Real Action

RR#11 TAKEAWAYS

If there's considerably more room for joy in your life, here are some fun ways to start exercising the joy muscle again.

EXERCISE #1 Place a check mark next to the ones you would be willing to do.

❏ Schedule a time right now to take a long walk, and really notice the world around you. Smell it, see it, hear it, and breathe it in.

❏ Think back to a movie, comedian, incident, or memory that tickled your funny bone and made you laugh. Relive the joy, laughter, smiles, and giggles with someone you love.

❏ Write down three things that weigh you down and prevent you from—or seem to justify—being less joyful. Referring to each thing, finish the sentence, "When it comes to this issue, I'd be more joyful if . . ."

❏ Explore new, less outcome-oriented ways to show (and make) love to your partner.

EXERCISE #2 Make a list of everything you consider to be a blessing in your life.

EXERCISE #3 Try one of the following to exercise your joy muscles.

- Treat yourself to a simple pleasure. Sometimes all it takes is some pampering (a hot bath, massage, etc.) to activate pleasure.

- Volunteer doing an activity that brings you joy—coaching a sports team, teaching a dance class, or taking your kids and their friends on a fun hike, field trip, or playdate.

- Make it a point to smile, sigh, and laugh more. Studies have shown that smiling, sighing, and laughing release endorphins (our body's natural painkillers), and serotonin, which elevates our moods.

Real Rule #12

A BREAKDOWN CAN BE
A BREAKTHROUGH:
Authentically Navigating a Crisis

Until now, I've talked primarily about navigating personal crises. In this chapter, however, we're going to deal with the kinds of crises that have a profound impact on who we are in the world—and how to turn an external breakdown into a breakthrough.

Not long ago, I got a phone call from a close friend at 3 A.M. She had just received an e-mail from me, saying I was "on my way to England to help a bereaved family member and desperately needed money to pay for the trip."

The catch? I hadn't sent an e-mail. She knew me well enough to know I never would and that I was the victim of an Internet scam.

What unfolded over the next few days was one of the most embarrassing and unsettling things I'd ever been through. My e-mail account had been compromised; hackers had accessed my contact list and sent out this phony letter to my database of over 1,000 people, soliciting money from clients I do business with, bereaved families from all over the world, old classmates—every imaginable person I've had contact with in the last 10 to 15 years.

And the worst part was: they erased the entire contact list after they sent out the e-mails. I had no way of notifying my friends, colleagues, and acquaintances that it was NOT me—that this was a scam.

It was horrific: people I knew and loved were going to be duped into sending money to wherever these criminals were instructing them to send it. In the name of caring about me and wanting to be there for me in a time of need, they were going to be swindled into sending money. I felt such a deep sense of violation—not to mention helplessness and humiliation—that something like this had happened.

So at 3 A.M., I started reconstructing my contact list, trying to remember whatever addresses I could and asking for help to fill in the blanks. Then I launched an intensive campaign of phone calls and e-mails to notify people that the e-mail was a scam. I contacted the local FBI, the San Diego District Attorney's office, the police department in London (where the money was supposed to be wired), as well as the fraud departments at Western Union and AOL.

As I'd feared, there were a few people who were going to send money as the e-mail requested. But what I hadn't expected was that, in the middle of my nightmare, I had one of the sweetest experiences of my life. The first day after the e-mails were sent, my phone didn't stop ringing. I had people calling me from all over the world, saying, "Ken, are you all right?" "Ken, we love you. What can we send?"

Those street-smart friends who immediately recognized it as a scam started calling to joke with me. Each phone call was funnier than the next. A woman friend of mine who recently got divorced and went back to college told me, "I knew it wasn't you—anybody who would ask a recently divorced college student for money is out of their mind!" Another buddy called and said, "Don't worry—I sent $2 million. Hope you're having fun in England!" After a while, I started answering the phone with, "Scam central! Can I help you?"

Old friends I hadn't spoken to in 10 to 15 years called, saying, "This gives me a great excuse to say hello and tell you that I miss you." Old consulting clients whose names were on the list called to say, "You know, I've been thinking about having you come back and do some work for our company. Are you available?" Suddenly, I was generating new business, refreshing old friendships, having these wonderful catch-up phone calls with people I hadn't spoken to in years, and breathing fresh air into a spontaneous network of love and support that I'd been building for more than a decade—all because of an e-mail scam!

Now, I'd be lying if I said the ordeal didn't continue. But in the middle of the nightmare was a lot of love and affection. I answered about a hundred phone calls that day; got close to 400 e-mails from people expressing their concern. It was a mixed blessing. Most of us don't ever get that outpouring of love and affection until the day of our funeral!

What's the moral of my story? Sometimes, just when it looks like the ship is going down, it's not. Faced with a full-blown crisis or the threat of one, take a deep breath and do everything you can to stop the bleeding. Look the sources of embarrassment straight in the eye with integrity, courage, and even a sense of humor. And don't be surprised if somehow, some way, the lemon turns to lemonade.

Real Rule #12: A Breakdown Can Be a Breakthrough. But only if you know how to authentically navigate a crisis. Say your "aw, shit"s. Get it all out. Then, take a deep breath. Stand tall. Don't get caught up in the drama. And then, take action to correct the problem as much as possible by making integrity-based decisions. Remember that, even at the appearance of impropriety, nobody can take your honor or integrity without your permission.

Johnson & Johnson: Extra-Strength Integrity

The classic case of integrity-based decision making and effective damage control taught in many of the world's top business schools is that of the Johnson & Johnson Tylenol crisis. In 1982, seven people in Chicago died from ingesting Extra-Strength Tylenol capsules laced with cyanide. Authorities determined that the tampering did not occur at the factory, but after the pills had been distributed at stores. Despite the extensive media coverage the case received, the murderer was never found.

Though Johnson & Johnson, the company that manufactures Tylenol, was absolved from blame, they had a major consumer crisis on their hands. The nationwide scare prompted copycat incidents, and the

FDA counted 270 incidents of suspected product tampering within the month. Tylenol was Johnson & Johnson's most profitable product, and suddenly, people were terrified to purchase it. Marketing experts from all over the country claimed that Johnson & Johnson would never be able to sell another product under the Tylenol brand name.

Boy, were they wrong. Not only did Johnson & Johnson stage a major comeback; they executed what many consider to be the finest example in recent history of big business responding ethically when disaster strikes.

Their first step was to put consumer safety first (and company profit second). Using major media outlets, they alerted consumers across the nation not to consume any type of Tylenol product until the extent of tampering could be determined. They issued a nationwide product recall—a total of 31 million bottles of Tylenol were pulled off the shelves and burned, causing an estimated loss of more than $100 million. The company went one step further, offering to exchange all Tylenol capsules that had already been purchased for Tylenol tablets instead.

Then came the second step of Johnson & Johnson's PR plan: to reinstate the integrity of their product and company. After proving to the world that they were genuinely committed to ensuring consumer safety, the company unleashed an extensive marketing and promotional program to bring Tylenol back to its number one spot. James E. Burke, the company chairman, said, "It will take time, it will take money, and it will be very difficult, but we consider it a moral imperative, as well as good business, to restore Tylenol to its preeminent position."

Less than six weeks after the deaths in Chicago, the company launched a new line of Tylenol capsules, this time with new triple-seal tamper-resistant packaging. The new packages appeared on shelves the following month, making Johnson & Johnson the first company to respond to the FDA's national mandate for tamper-resistant packaging. They also issued a series of coupons and discounts, in addition to making millions of presentations to the medical community and launching a new advertising campaign.

Getting Real—"Ethical Business"

In the era following the Enron scandal and Bernie Madoff's epic Ponzi scheme, it's easy to accuse big business of being invariably corrupt. And to Occupy Wall Street in a show of outrage and protest for the financial injustices being perpetuated in our nation. Fortunately, there are thousands of businesses in the United States and beyond that still champion a strict code of business ethics. Yours is no doubt among them.

Today, nearly 30 years later, the Tylenol brand is as strong as ever. Most people don't think twice about taking a box of Extra-Strength Tylenol capsules off the shelf at their neighborhood CVS. That's because Johnson & Johnson responded swiftly, smartly, and—most important— responsibly to the crisis in 1982. They behaved with integrity and resolve, never succumbing to the temptation to cast blame.

Now compare that to the way Toyota handled their PR crisis in 2010. Talk about opposite ends of the spectrum! For more than 30 years, Toyota had had a sterling reputation for reliability. In 2009, there were 356,000 Camrys sold in the U.S., making it the top-selling car in the nation. The Corolla was second in line, with sales of almost 297,000.

But the trust that Toyota spent years building decayed rapidly. After reports of gas pedals sticking and causing unintended acceleration in the Prius, Toyota did begin massive recalls and halted sales of certain vehicles in their product line. The real problem, however, was in the way they handled the crisis . . . or, to be more accurate, the way they did not handle it.

Apparently, problems with the Prius pedals were first reported in 2008, but the company dragged its feet when it came to addressing them. A variety of sources claim that Toyota likely had information on the defects long before the problem even hit the public arena, which means they may have been able to prevent the many accidents, injuries, and deaths that occurred.

Toyota's response to the media outcry was lethargic at best, totally unresponsive at worst. They shifted the blame onto the individual drivers and onto the states where accidents more frequently occur—anywhere but themselves. Public trust in the company plummeted. Sales of competitive vehicles that have long struggled in second, third, fourth, and fifth place all rose. While it's too soon to tell, the brand name that has long been preferred by millions may never recover.

And this is from a company world-famous for having long-term strategic growth plans that stretch 50, 100, or even 200 years into the future, depending on whom you ask. On what page, one wonders, of Toyota's 100-year plan, do they discuss the idea of destroying in six months what took decades to build?

When it comes to preserving your reputation and behaving in a way that is ethical and responsible, who would you rather be—Tylenol or Toyota?

Take Action

We all know the saying, "It takes a lifetime to build a reputation and a few minutes to destroy it." One wrong step or a few careless words can cause irreversible damage. Toyota may have a rich legacy of well-made cars, but all it takes is a nationwide PR crisis for that legacy to be toppled in no time at all.

In the noncorporate realm, however, it's not always so cut and dry. In this day and age, hits to our reputation are often out of our control. We live in a world of tabloids, identity theft, rumormongers, e-mail hackers, scam artists, and political assassins. Whether you are CEO or a girl in middle school who has aroused the ire of an archenemy, your reputation can be destroyed in mere moments, with a few clicks of a mouse.

I have never hesitated to ask for donations for my daughter's non-profit foundation, the Jenna Druck Center—in fact I've been our biggest fundraiser. But I've never taken a penny for myself, and never will. So when I discovered that insidious e-mail circulating through my contact list, asking people to send me money, I was devastated. The scammers had compromised the very things I hold most precious—my reputation, my integrity, my name—by trying to dupe a thousand of my friends, family members, clients, colleagues, and others into sending money.

Getting Real—"Internet Fraud"

The FBI recently published a news report that Internet fraud cost $559 million in 2009 (double the amount from cyber-crime in 2008). Protect yourself from hackers, phishing scams, and identity theft by taking as many precautions as possible. If you do get scammed, do the best you can to quickly control the damage.

Real Rule #12 imparts two valuable life lessons. First, we're all vulnerable. Whether it's an Internet scam, being cheated by a business partner, or a vicious rumor being spread in your community, you may very well be falsely accused, attacked, or suspected of wrongdoing at some point in your life. Each of us is susceptible; no one is immune.

The second lesson is: if you are the victim of a scam or a lie, or if you do actually screw up, then it's up to you to do something about it. Like Johnson & Johnson, you've got to do all you can to make things right when there is the appearance of impropriety—even if you did absolutely nothing wrong. That requires taking two swift actions.

Action #1 is full disclosure. Your first responsibility in any crisis: secure the safety and well-being of others first. Disclose that something has been compromised, whether it's a bottle of Tylenol or an e-mail list. Do everything that's humanly possible to limit or minimize the damage. That means being honest with people if something presents a danger to their well-being, and then giving them very specific instructions for how to protect themselves. It also means taking the hit if you actually *have* done something wrong.

In my particular situation, it was the financial well-being of my friends and colleagues that was at stake. My foremost goal was to contact everyone I could think of who might have been in my contact list, tell them it was a scam, and instruct them not to send money. It had nothing to do with my embarrassment or reputation. My goal was to do whatever I could to protect people from being exploited.

So I pulled out the stops, stayed up all night, and tried to find and notify each person who had been contacted. Without a contact list, it was no easy task; I devoted several days to nothing but phone calls and e-mails, trying to touch base with hundreds of people. My e-mail was brief and to the point, but I took responsibility and apologized for any inconvenience the situation may have caused. I needed to assure some of these people that their relationship with me or my company did not present any kind of liability to them.

The fact was that my account was hacked. I had a responsibility to protect the financial, physical, and spiritual well-being of the people on my contact list. I wanted to let them know I was accountable, and that I had reported the fraud to all the appropriate authorities (FBI, local police, AOL scam unit, etc.). I took every step to limit the damage, which meant I was up for 40 hours straight on the phone and computer. It was exhausting, but so worth it in the end.

Once you've done all you can to "stop the bleeding," it's time for Action #2: Prevention. For Johnson & Johnson, that meant protecting the health and safety of their customers above all else to ensure that there were no more accidental deaths. For me, it meant finding ways to prevent something like this from ever happening again. So I took my computer into the shop and had it completely reworked—they combed the hard drive, checked for bugs, and installed the best virus software plan money could buy. Then, I followed up with the local police, FBI, FCA, AOL, and Western Union to see how, in a world that's awakening to all the new threats to our security and privacy, I could help prevent this from happening to others.

When disaster strikes, take responsibility. Protecting your integrity— whether personal or professional—is your job, no one else's. Apologize for what happened, and back your words with action. Do something that has a direct impact on the situation so that people not only know that you care, but that you've taken action to prevent the same thing from happening again. Continue to look for opportunities to make things right, do your best to turn the lemon into lemonade, and make peace with the things you cannot change.

Protecting Your Integrity

Have you ever heard the story of Raymond Donovan, the U.S. Secretary of Labor during the Reagan administration? In 1987, he and six other defendants were indicted by a grand jury for allegedly hiring a company owned by a Genovese crime family to construct a new subway line in New York City.

After a five-year trial—yes, you read that correctly, *five* years in and out of court—Donovan and his fellow defendants were acquitted. Completely exonerated. Set free. That's when Donovan issued his famous quote to the press: "Which office do I go to get my reputation back?"

It's sad but true: once your reputation has been tarnished, it's an uphill battle to reinstate it. On a far less publicized level, many of us face attacks on our character at some time in our lives. Despite all I've done to mitigate the effects of the scammer, I am still doing damage control with people I run into. I definitely took a hit.

Getting Real—"The Bark of Reputation"

How difficult it is to save the bark of reputation
from the rocks of ignorance. — Petrarch

It's a pretty helpless feeling. In the beginning I felt like I should have known better. I hadn't downloaded the latest version of spyware; how could I be so irresponsible? If only I had just bought a Mac. But, as the FBI informed me, no matter what precautions we take, there are people who will still be able to compromise our safety and our integrity. No matter what we do, we're vulnerable to scams, spams, and viruses. Pulling the guilt, shame, or "I told you so" card doesn't help us or anybody else. That said, there's no reason we shouldn't do everything we can to protect ourselves and those we care about by taking advantage of reliable safety and security precautions.

As I learned, you can't always protect your computer, or your reputation. There will be times in life when you take a hit. Your integrity, however, can stand strong and resolute through the roughest of storms. And you can limit some of the damage. Though they are closely connected, reputation and integrity are different animals. Your reputation may take hits over the course of your life, from e-mail scams and business failures to vicious rumors or damaging gossip.

Your integrity, however, is harder to attack. Regardless of what others say, the heart of who you are remains the same.

The people who have trust and faith in you—the people who know your integrity—will withhold judgment when you're accused of a crime or transgression. They are the ones who know you, trust you, and hold you as innocent until proven guilty. They won't listen to the lies or slander or falsehoods or allegations others may perpetuate. They know that you are a good person because you have earned their trust and respect over time.

Even if you've established your integrity, strengthening and securing it over the years, you may be called into question when something unexpected or damaging happens. But if you accept responsibility, take swift action, and do everything in your power to right the wrong, your integrity will be reinstated and reinforced. At the end of the day, your reputation may be bruised, but your trustworthiness and value to others will remain intact.

We are taught our whole lives to view breakdowns as destructive and counterproductive mishaps. But sometimes a breakdown leads to a breakthrough. When things take a turn for the worse, when we screw up or get caught in a bad situation, our character is tested. It is nothing less than a moment of truth. We make a definitive statement about the person we are. We may choose to cover it up, blame others, justify our actions, make excuses, or deny responsibility. Or, we may choose to assume responsibility for what happened, take the hit, apologize, and do whatever we can to rectify our mistakes. The choice is ours, and it defines our integrity. We are either honest and trustworthy, remorseful and responsible, humble and apologetic—or not. If we navigate the crisis with honesty, courage, humility, and respect, we can often stop further damage, face into the adversity, and fortify our character.

Real Action

RR#12 TAKEAWAYS

EXERCISE #1 Nobody asks for crisis to strike, but it happens all the same. If you're facing a crisis in your life, whether it's personal or professional, which of the following action steps would you take?

- Take responsibility for your part in the crisis.

- Protect your integrity and that of the others involved.

- Apologize for what happened, and back your words with action.

- Do what you can to come up with a workable solution—to "stop the bleeding," so to speak.

- Take preventative measures to prevent the crisis from happening again.

EXERCISE #2 Identify a time in your life when there was a crisis or breakdown. How do you rate your handling of the situation on a scale from 1 to 10 (10 being "handled with 100 percent effectiveness")? What would you do differently knowing what you know today?

Real Rule #13

REAL VALUE HAS NO DOLLAR SIGNS:
Self-Worth and the Currency of Love

Success isn't about dollars. Your worth as a human being can't be measured in numbers—it's about another kind of wealth. The wealth of loving, caring relationships you have with other human beings in your life. This isn't news, of course, but I have found that while widely known, this Real Rule is commonly neglected.

The slogan "your network is your net worth" has been around for years. But saying it and believing it are two different things. Despite all the "people-are-your-greatest-asset" hype, many still consider money to be their greatest asset. Meanwhile, the relationships in their life get lower priority and less investment.

How do you measure success? Is it how much money you have in the bank? Is it status (i.e., where you live, the car you drive, the position you hold)? If the answer comes with a dollar sign, you may want to reconsider your wealth-building plan, portfolio, and priorities. At the end of your life, what do you truly want to have accomplished? I've never heard of anybody lying on their deathbed saying, "I wish I'd worked harder, closed bigger deals, and made more money . . ."

Real Rule #13: Real Value Has No Dollar Signs. Sometimes creating good faith, love, trust, and value (without any financial gain) results in the best kind of net worth. Relationship worth can mean staying at home and spending extra time with the family, or investing more deeply in a marriage that's going through a rough spot when it would be a lot easier to just turn and run. It means staying up with a sick friend to hold their hand, or working late to help a colleague with a challenging project. It's the unconditional love you give your parents as they age (even if they are becoming more ornery) and the day-to-day affection you show your children as they grow up.

These are the actions that produce *real* wealth. For me, "real wealth" means living with a full heart. Knowing there are people in my life who I love and who love me. Having faith we can work through whatever differences may arise (and they do). And feeling a deep sense of gratitude that I get to share the journey with them. My daughter, Stefie, who I see or text message every day, and with whom I have a deep and wonderful connection. My nephew Scott and his beautiful two-year-old daughter, Alexandra, who I get to see thriving, each in their own way. My mother, Roslyn, almost 90, who sends me loving e-mails when she knows I'm stressed out. My beloved, Lisette, with whom I get to share every difficult and glorious day of my life. Our sweet and goofy rescue dog, Bean, who puts a smile on my face. And my dear friends, each of whom touch my heart in a special way with their love. Each of these relationships brings out the best and most loving parts of me, fills me up and enriches my life. I am a wealthy man—people-rich. And I feel blessed.

The investment we make with our generosity, forgiveness, affection, patience, and humility may someday make us "people-rich" beyond our wildest dreams.

So why is it that so many people still have a hard time understanding that money isn't the answer? Why do we still go searching for our self-worth in our bank accounts and status symbols like cars, houses, clothes, and where our kids go to school?

It's hard to quantify value in a relationship. How do we really know we're good parents, or good partners, or good managers? It's not something that shows up on a quarterly statement. Money, on the other hand, is very concrete. There's a profit margin and a bottom line. It's easy to scan the right-hand column and figure out exactly where you stand. When it comes to our finances, we operate in a clear-cut world of exchange: you do the work, you get the money. It's easier to define ourselves by the tangible evidence of our success than by intangibles such as "feeling loved," "being connected," or "feeling understood."

Getting Real—"True Value"

According to the French playwright Molière, "Things only have the value that we give them." If you assign that value to your relationships instead of things, you'll be a far richer person.

Money also buys status, which is comfortingly measurable. Some people assume that if they buy the hottest car or the most expensive jewelry, their worth will be greater in other people's eyes. Such symbols of status can give a temporary "hit" of self-worth, as if filling the hole in our lives left by a lack of meaningful, truly intimate relationships. But as we all know, self-soothing with status and self-medicating with money is a short-lived "fix." In the end, it's never enough!

We all know people who have more money than they know what to do with—and are absolutely miserable. The symbols of material prosperity do not make us *feel* wealthy. Our internal "net worth" can be found in our "bank of relationships." Many of my clients have found themselves emotionally bankrupt after a life spent trying to buy friends and family ties. At the end of the day, they're sitting in their 15,000-square-foot mansions, wondering why they feel so empty and alone. As an executive coach, I have had the good fortune of being able to help many of these very successful but unhappy men and women turn things around and discover a world of personal wealth and fulfillment that reaches far beyond money, property, and status.

Because real wealth, as many of my clients have come to realize, has surprisingly little to do with money. Sure, we all get caught up in the money game. We have bills to pay and jobs to do. No one can argue that we don't need money to survive. Those among us who are entrepreneurs have mountains to climb and empires to conquer—and money helps. (A little status in the eyes of the people you respect never hurts.) But money should be a means to an end, never the end itself. For all the worth we attach to money, it's worthless when it comes to real, sustainable happiness and prosperity.

After Jenna died, it became overwhelmingly clear to me that love is the only real currency. All the money in the world would not have meant anything to me. Luckily you don't have to experience a significant life loss to begin rethinking your definition of wealth.

Deathbed Confessions and Awakenings

Take a quick trip into your imagination—a step into the future. Your deathbed confessions. What do you imagine yourself saying to your loved ones at the end of your own life?

I doubt it will have anything to do with the size of your bank account. It will probably be more along the lines of, "I wish I'd spent more time with my kids," "I wish I'd told my dad I loved him," "I wish I could have worked things out with my ex," or, "I wish I had let go and danced more." Whatever it is for you, that's your new bottom line.

This "deathbed" exercise helps crystallize what is truly important in your life. What is precious and irreplaceable? What ultimately holds the greatest value? What gives you the greatest satisfaction? The answers will most always pertain to three things: your relationships with the people you love; the unexplored, unexpressed parts of yourself; and the yearning for greater freedom and peace.

We are each given so many teachable moments in our life, moments where we can access a fuller understanding of life's Real Rules. You may be standing in one right now, which is why you picked up this book. Perhaps the door to greater awareness has been flung open wide. Maybe it's just barely been cracked. Either way, it's time to reevaluate your priorities and restructure your life accordingly.

Real personal wealth, I discovered, is not about what you get, but what you give—without expecting anything in return. Some people call this kind of selfless giving "service," others "philanthropy" or "tithing." Since starting the Jenna Druck Center and launching its Families Helping Families and Young Women's Leadership programs 15 years ago, I have given of myself, heart and soul, 24/7, to countless families and young women. We have raised millions of nonprofit dollars. Even though not a penny of it has gone into my own pocket, I feel like the richest "dude" in San Diego.

Honoring the life and spirit of my angel daughter—being the "the keeper of her legacy"—was not what I had signed up for as a father. But it's what I got. Being a lifeline to bereaved families and empowering young women was a way of turning my pain into love—and then giving that love away. Over time, it became my mission. And a rich source of knowledge about the Real Rules of Life.

It doesn't have to take a tragedy or disaster to bring out the compassion and philanthropy in us. Sure, our compassion is awakened when we become firsthand witnesses to devastating, horrific losses. Even the most miserly among us are moved to lend a helping hand. But we need not wait. There is suffering all around us, in our own communities, neighborhoods, families, nations, and around the world. We don't have to wait for a tragedy or disaster to give of ourselves. We have the ability to reach down into the wellspring of compassion and generously volunteer our time, talent, and/or treasury to help an individual, family, cause, or organization that, like the Jenna Druck Center, is devoted to relieving human suffering and uplifting the human spirit.

There are simple things you can do to awaken and begin to cultivate real wealth today. Subtle changes make a profound difference. It may mean starting or ending each day differently—perhaps with the gift of meditation, gentle yoga, prayer, music, or a walk. It could be as simple as instituting a family dinner and movie night with your kids. Perhaps it's joining a tantalizing book club with your friends or having a weekly date night with your spouse.

In a way that speaks personally to you, establish the kinds of activities, practices and routines that reflect your commitment to the people in your life and to your own well-being. Cultivate the conditions for real wealth by aligning yourself with those things that afford a more deeply satisfying experience of peace, connection, gratitude, forgiveness, generosity, and love.

Getting Real—"Cultivating the Conditions"

Cultivating the conditions for real wealth means giving freely of two things: your time, and your heart.

So many of us live from impulse to impulse, day in and day out. Buy the nice car, get the promotion, and splurge on the vacation. But the moment we see someone who understands real value, we quickly recognize the void in our own lives. We see it in their eyes. And their relationships. The simple joy they're experiencing is so obvious—it's in their smile, their ease, their sense of peace. The closeness in their family or in their marriage, the kindness they exude or the ease with which their company operates.

They're living out Real Rule #13, doing things every day that provide more enduring peace, satisfaction, and purpose, and that strengthen the intimate relationships in their lives.

Don't you deserve the same?

$$\diamondsuit \quad \diamondsuit \quad \diamondsuit$$

Real Action

RR#13 TAKEAWAYS

Real value comes from the people in your life, not material possessions or money in the bank. The way you "cash in" on that value is by cultivating your heart and your relationships.

EXERCISE #1 Check the suggestions you like for mining real wealth in your life:

- ❑ Surprise your partner with an unexpected picnic lunch or romantic dinner out—followed by a fun shared activity.

- ❑ Clear your schedule (at least) one night a week and spend it with your family doing something intimate, like reading, or something adventurous, like making a family movie together.

- ❑ Call an old friend just to see how they are and share a sweet memory.

- ❑ Slip a note into a loved one's pocket telling him or her how much they mean to you (or a stone marked with "I love you" on it).

- ❑ Unplug your home phone (or power down your iPhone!) next time you have a heart-to-heart conversation with a family member.

❏ Do something special for your mom or dad—make them breakfast in bed, treat them to a massage, or take them out for coffee.

❏ Plan a get-together with your friends and family, and instead of crowding around the TV, talk to each other.

EXERCISE # 2 List three sources of real wealth in your life and at least one thing you could do to make each of them a greater priority.

EXERCISE #3 If you're not already doing so, sign up to volunteer, make a donation, or perform an act of kindness for a worthy person or a cause without expecting anything in return—and bask in the warmth of real wealth that flows back to you.

Real Rule #14

YOU'VE GOTTA HAVE SKIN IN THE GAME:
Taking Risks, Investing Yourself

You've heard of getting your head in the game. But what about having skin in the game?

The great investor Warren Buffett, whom I have had the pleasure of meeting, coined the term. It originated in the context of an investment strategy—high-ranking executives are supposed to buy stock in the organization they lead. Executives can talk all they want, but the best vote of confidence is to put their own money on the line. In other words: if they really believe in it, the top dogs should have a stake in their own company.

When I talk about Real Rule #14, I'm not just talking about Warren or Wall Street. I'm talking about every area of your life. It's just as true at home as it is in the office. Because until you have skin in the game, until you have something of great personal value invested, you're not really playing.

How many of us play it safe in our relationships? We put little or nothing on the line, never really opening ourselves up to the other person out of fear of getting hurt. How many of us play it safe at work? We do the bare minimum, just enough to collect the paycheck. And yet, the highest and best expression of who we are comes only when we learn to overcome our fears and allow ourselves to risk and to care.

It's not about your investment portfolio. It's about investing yourself.

Just as investors can't buy stocks with a stranger's money, you can't expect anyone else to assume the risk for you. Unless you make your own sacrifices, you're never going to harvest the rich, resonant rewards life has to offer. Or the pride of ownership that comes with hard work and putting something of consequence (i.e., time, money, passion, faith) on the line. Ask yourself: What have I really put into this? What is my commitment here? If you are sincerely committed, the answer should be, "Everything!"

If you have lost sight of what it is you really care about, or what would be worth such an investment, you may be overdue for a "passion checkup." Finding out what genuinely motivates you, what you really care about, and recharging your batteries can be as simple as asking yourself, "What would I do every day if money were no object?" "What would be the best thing that could happen to me?" "What in my life is worth fighting for?" Or "What would it kill me to lose?"

The sweetest pleasures and delights the universe has in store for you come from putting your whole heart into the things that are truly important. Your relationships, job, kids, and marriage; your community, faith, country, and/or vision (big or small) for making the world a better place.

Getting Real—"Fake It 'Til You Make It"

A lot of people are just going through the motions. "Fake it 'til you make it," the saying goes. The motions are empty unless you've got your skin in the game—unless you've invested something that shows the depth of your commitment.

Are you living purposefully and passionately, or are you just going through the motions? Are you taking risks? Are you dumbed down, or even paralyzed, by fear? Do you hide out in a job and/or marriage of convenience? Might you be insulating yourself from pain, failure, and disappointment by acting indifferent and aloof?

Or, are you living passionately and with conviction? To more deeply dedicate yourself to living your dream, to live your life and not some diluted version of winning everyone's approval, you must begin to put more skin in the game.

This is your life, your ride. Make it count! Believe in it! Invest in it! Do the things that really matter! The rewards will be so much sweeter and longer-lasting than getting people's approval or just going through the motions.

This is also your world!

Once we awaken to the Real Rules that affect our individual lives, we can look at the world beyond our own self-interest. Awakening to the needs, callings, injustices, inequities, and threats to our families, friends, communities, regions, and planet—and addressing them—is also part of having skin in the game.

Nowhere is this more true than in our current planetary crisis. Our collective hunger for consumption and acquisition (oil, food, water, power, status, religion, etc.) has been likened to that of an out-of-control addict who would sooner destroy themselves than be denied "a fix." Unless and until we sober up and realize what we're doing is destructive and unsustainable, there will come a time when the damage will be irreversible. For an alcoholic, that point happens when the liver and kidneys begin failing. For a planet, it's when fossil fuels destroy our air and water, animals become extinct, war becomes imminent, and greedy human hearts cease to care.

Addiction is the disease of denial. So is out-of-control consumption, pollution, waste, and spending. Nothing is ever enough. In either case, things end badly. Until we awaken to what's at risk when we trash our bodies, or our ecosystems, we'll remain in a dumbed-down state. Like the addict, we'll hide, deny, repress, justify, excuse, dismiss, disassociate, and explain away the dangers and disparities. Which, in turn, will justify not having to change anything.

Unless we set the alarm and put some skin in the game, we will sleep through all the wake-up calls. Until we personally dedicate ourselves to a new approach—talk to the man in the mirror and make a change, as Michael Jackson so eloquently said in his song—the fear and denial will surely prevail.

This past year, one of my consulting clients, Sid, the semiretired founder and CEO of a thriving family business, took a long, hard look in the mirror. For several years, Sid had dismissed the thought of doing a "green audit," as his two sons called it, on his food services company. There were many things they could do to be more eco-friendly. And some of his competitors had actually taken those steps. But Sid didn't want to do anything that might put his master plan (retiring and leaving the family business to his sons) at risk. It was his dream.

The subject of becoming more eco-friendly came up spontaneously during one of our quarterly Family Council Meetings. I took the opportunity to tell Sid and his sons about the Native American ideal, called "Seventh Generation." "All the decisions that were made," I explained, "took into consideration the effects on families seven generations from now. It was their most sacred value and guided all their decisions."

The week following our Family Council Meeting, Sid called me to schedule some individual time. He'd been doing a lot of thinking and explained, "Ken, for a long time, I believed there was too much at risk to change things around in our company. Especially in this economy. But now, I want to do something. While I have the chance, I want to improve the lives of my children's children's children."

Sid explained that he had already spoken to his wife and sons and they had decided to invest a considerable amount of money over several years to make their company green. He ended our meeting tearfully by telling me that he was "very happy and very proud of what they had done."

It's your life. Your world. Are you up for cultivating a new and wonderful vision of sustainability, compassion, and peace? And for putting some skin in the game?

✦ ✦ ✦

Real Action

RR#14 TAKEAWAYS

EXERCISE #1 What fears might be holding you back from investing more of yourself in your job, marriage, parenting, friendships, career? Name them!

EXERCISE #2 Next to each fear describe an action that would help free you from that fear and solidify your decision to risk something to get something,

EXERCISE #3 There are big differences between "foolish" risks and "smart" risks.
Looking at a situation in your current life, write down examples of each.

EXERCISE #4 List three things you care about so deeply, or are so passionate about, that you'd be willing to risk it all for them.

EXERCISE #5 If you are risk-aversive or risk-avoidant, describe three things you could do to build your courage and confidence.

Real Rule #15

TAKING HONEST INVENTORY:
Overcoming Our Blind Spots

B lind spots. We all have them. And not just in the rearview mirror of our cars. Like insecurities and distortions in the way we perceive things, blind spots they come with the territory of being human. By recognizing your blind spots and taking action to offset them, you get to see what you would have missed, correct what you would have skewed, and choose from clarity instead of fear. This is what I call "taking honest inventory."

One blind spot that needs self-management is the ego. The truth is, most of us are more egotistical than we think. We may never admit it to anyone, but we frequently place ourselves and our beliefs at the center of the universe. Families, companies, and entire nations are too often guided by unspoken rules and politics that exist solely to accommodate the egos of a select few "leaders" or "ideologies." We have seen the results when people in power need to feel especially important, superior, and indispensable. But no matter who we are, all of us suffer to some degree from the tyranny of our own egos.

Here's the problem. When we live, breathe, act, and speak from our ego, we end up acting in ways that are detrimental to our own success—

and to the well-being of the people and institutions to which we have devoted our lives. By catering to the whims of our egos and insecurities—and by remaining unaware—we're actually shooting ourselves, our families, and our organizations in the proverbial foot.

One of my coaching clients, Steve, used to be a prime example of this. As the CEO of a large biotech company where he had worked for more than 20 years, he was the classic example of a micromanager, controlling every aspect of his organization. Like so many high-powered executives, he needed to be reminded to trust the men and women he had gone to great lengths and expense to recruit and train.

At the company's annual management retreat, which I facilitate, Steve was prepared to give the same motivational speech he'd been giving for almost a decade. It's the same tack some of us take with our kids—pounding in the same message, again and again. Like an overbearing parent who didn't trust that his kids had understood the first time, Steve began his pounding speech. His team of high-powered scientists, necks craned upward to the boss, began tuning him out as they always had. As I sat there listening, I wondered about his management team. If empowered to do so, might they have created their own version of his annual speech, one that would have been more effective and actionable than anything he'd yet imagined?

The following day, I spoke to Steve. After some time, he agreed to contain his impulse to lead every discussion and dictate the direction of every brainstorming session—and let his management team guide the day instead. I offered to bring duct tape to the session in case that would help, but he assured me he could keep his agreement to stand back! I reminded him that his teammates and all the people he had hired were extremely skilled and capable. Not only that, but they were champing at the bit to put some skin in the game and take some ownership and responsibility for getting results.

And that's exactly what happened. With their new freedom, his management team took over. For the first time in literally ten years, the retreat room was buzzing with ideas and excitement. People were interacting and collaborating; there was lively debate and discussion. Certain leaders stood out, and their readiness was evident. Suddenly what would have been just another nuts and bolts retreat was transformed into a dynamic, creative, and productive meeting that took on a momentum which continues today, a year later.

At the debriefing with Steve's management team, they were beaming with pride and declared the annual retreat "the best ever." Steve, on the other hand, took me aside and sulked, "Well, I guess I'm not needed around here anymore."

That sad statement confirmed what was really going on. For years, Steve had been living with the insecurity and fear of being dispensable and unworthy as a leader. His behavior and decisions were dictated more by his need to feel important, powerful, competent, and in control than by what was actually good for his team and the company. He was feeding his own shaky ego, putting his agenda above everyone else's to prove his mettle as a CEO. But it was hurting his company and creating a culture of dependency and detachment.

Real Rule #15 says: Everybody, including you, has blind spots. Steve had a big one that he just couldn't see. He was unknowingly compensating for feelings of unworthiness by being an overbearing leader. Once he recognized, and humbly accepted, the truth of this rule—and got out of the way—he unleashed his management team's full potential. Ironically, he unleashed his own efficacy as a leader in the process.

Like Steve, we do ourselves a disservice when we cover our insecurities with arrogance, bravado, and intimidation. We lose credibility and effectiveness as leaders, parents, spouses, and members of our communities. The paradox of power is that strength comes from empowering others. The key to building strong organizations, being effective parents, and living the fullest, richest lives possible is learning to let go of our own egoic insecurities. When we do, we solidify our own sense of worth, empower others, and lead them (from behind) in getting exceptional results.

Pass the Ball!

I often tell CEO's to "think like Phil Jackson."

As a five-time champion NBA coach, Phil understands that less is more. The key to the Lakers' success is that he has created authentic relationships with each man on his team. He empowers his players by allowing them to engage in the process of playing basketball and have a sense of ownership as a result. That's the way you bring out the best in people. It's also the way you create purpose and meaning, and the way you engender motivation and loyalty in the people who work (or play) for you.

It works much the same way in an office environment. As a leader, it's your job to give opportunity and responsibility to the members of your team—in other words, to distribute (i.e., delegate) the ball. In basketball lingo, "You've got to know how to be the point guard rather than the center." Or, in corporate talk, good leaders bring out the best in their team by creating opportunities for each member to show his or her special skills and demonstrate what they can do to help the organization meet its goals.

Getting Real—"Teamwork"

Vince Lombardi was right about a lot of things, including this: "Individual commitment to a group effort—that's what makes a team work, a company work, a society work, a civilization work."

Take Kobe Bryant. Nobody doubts that Kobe can sink almost every shot he takes. And at the beginning of his career, that's exactly what he did. But soon the other teams caught on, and assigned three people to hang on him in every game. Suddenly his team was underperforming. Phil Jackson knew that if he wanted the Lakers to win, he had to instill a sense of teamwork in Kobe. So he sat him down and said, "Look, Kobe. You've got to figure out when it's your time to take the ball to the hole, but you've also got to figure out how to empower your teammates so they can take it there, too. Otherwise, we're never going to win a championship."

In my mind, the Lakers have won the several championships they've won because Jackson was able to influence Kobe's decision making. He helped Kobe see the benefit in bringing the greatness out of the other guys on his team (something Jackson himself learned from his coach, Red Holzman, in the 1970s when he was playing for the New York Knicks). The extent to which Kobe distributes the ball and involves his teammates is the extent to which the Lakers are successful. If this story sounds familiar, it's because Jackson had lived through it once before, with none other than Michael Jordan—a scoring machine who had learned the lesson Kobe learned, and won many championships.

Off the court and in our own lives, it can be hard to know when to pass the ball and when to take the shot. Striking the perfect balance between the two requires that our egos are in check and that we are doing what's best (not feeding on insecurity or greed) for the greater good. Because in each of our lives, there does come a time when we need to take things into our own hands. Whether you're a CEO, a parent, or the head of a community organization, there are certain decisions that only you can make. What makes a great leader is the ability to identify when making an executive decision is necessary—which is usually only 10 percent of the time—and when it's not.

For the other 90 percent of situations that arise, doing what's best for the company means engaging the right people and working as a team. The beauty is that when you take this approach, you can empower people who actually know more about the situation than you do! And in turn, they can make the necessary decisions from a position of expertise that you yourself may not have. Discussion, debates, and transparent conversations are almost always better than knee-jerk, trickle-down decisions that originate from a single mind or needy ego. Delegation, dialogue, and informed decision making help all of us arrive at the best solutions and results.

How many professional ballplayers never win a championship because they have no idea how to balance their own skill with that of their teammates? Perhaps they fear that allowing others around them to become great will diminish them. How many times does this also happen with corporate CEO's, elected officials, entertainers, parents, and community leaders whose egos are out of check?

Turning Spectators into Team Players

One of the most tragic losses a business can suffer is the loss of potential. Most often, this loss is incurred from the organization's greatest resource: its employees. To continue the basketball analogy, if you don't recognize and reward your team members, you're effectively turning them into spectators. This is true whether you're in the NBA or at an annual management retreat.

Getting Real—"Power With" instead of "Power Over"

Exhibiting "power with" is about empowering your family, friends, teammates, employees, or co-workers. "Power over" is about letting your ego run wild.

We have seen how one CEO from our earlier example, didn't know how to empower his people to be team players. By taking all the power for himself, he had unknowingly sapped his employees' motivation, undermined their creativity, and lowered their potential. Unfortunately, after 25 years of executive coaching with some of the world's top leaders in business and government—and their high-level management teams—I can say that this kind of egotistical behavior is not uncommon. Nor is it uncommon in the families I work with.

Acting like a Team—or a Family

We may call ourselves "teams" and "families," yet, we often don't behave that way. In this way, parenting and running a company can be strikingly similar. Consider a group of exceptionally talented employees (or children) who are sitting on their hands, looking up to see how they could please and impress their boss (or parents)—and how they can outdo one another in the process. This is not team-like or family-like behavior. Each may work hard and perform well as an individual, but the fact that they are walking around on eggshells, not wanting to rock the boat with one another, does not make for an effective work or family environment.

In a corporate setting, those who refuse to kiss up to the boss eventually rebel and leave. It's the same in a family. Much of the responsibility often rests on the shoulders of the boss and parents. Bosses and parents who never learn to share power with their employees or children, instead focusing on having power over them, set themselves up for struggle. As a result, none of the executives or children feels the courage to speak up, challenge, or disagree with the folks in charge. Nor do they feel the safety, freedom, or motivation to generate new energy, ideas, and enthusiasm. Leaders and parents who use their power to stifle instead of inspire are often unaware of what they're doing to flatten the energy in their companies and families. Sooner or later, they find themselves surrounded by compliant (secretly rebellious) subordinates or disconnected children. And they wonder why they feel all alone.

By getting our egos, insecurities, and blind spots out of the equation, a leader's or parent's potential for effectiveness increases, as does their level of engagement and morale. And this "empowerment effect," as I call it, begins to spread throughout the company or family.

Misuse of power comes at a high cost: whether it's the effectiveness, integrity, and productivity of an organization—or the disconnection and despair in a family. Kids and employees become disheartened when their leader/parent can't seem to get out of his or her own way. Or doesn't seem to care. Smart, talented people don't stick around very long in a place where they're not allowed to shine. Misuse of power also leads to passive-aggressive behavior and backstabbing behind closed doors. When people feel they have to resort to such measures to survive, there's a lot of infighting, office/family "politics," and positioning for favored status—i.e., stroking the bosses' or Mom's and Dad's egos. As a result, you have a weak and fragmented management team or family. And an elephant in the living- or boardroom.

Dysfunctional teams and families breed compliant people whose highest held values are security and conformity. They won't really speak out for fear that they're putting their jobs and promotional status, allowance, or privileges on the line. Instead of a culture of teamwork and entrepreneurship, you have a culture of intimidation, compliance, and fear. Without the capacity to talk things out and work together, problems are allowed to fester. Effectiveness is compromised. Little issues that could have been nipped in the bud by open communication, understanding, and clear agreements spread into larger infections, and eventually grow into organizational and familial dis-ease.

This is where resentment, and wrongful termination claims, begins to seep into the organization's framework. It's no small surprise that these are the kinds of businesses and families that are most susceptible to crises, and the most likely to suffer from long, drawn-out conflicts.

So what kind of preventive measures can you enact to protect yourself, your family, and your company from wasting time and opportunities? And harvesting the richness that effective teams and families are capable of providing? How do you take Real Rule #15 regarding blind spots, and turn it into an actionable plan? And where do you begin?

Steps to Prevent Unnecessary Losses

Working with healthy, vibrant, well-functioning companies and their CEO's on organizational effectiveness, I'm always looking for ways they can be proactive and preventive. It's the same with families. I start by asking two simple questions: What *conversations* do we need to be in to address the real issues facing your organization/family? Being in the right conversations is the key. Asking, "How can we act today to effectively address existing or potential crises, conflicts, opportunities, and threats in our organization/family?" The first step is to assess what's really going on. What's working? And what's not? Is there a mission, vision, and strategic plan that's been agreed on and that people in your company or family are aligned with? That includes making sure that every employee/family member knows what is expected of them, what the goals are, how to complement their colleagues/family members, and what it really means to work together. Getting people on the same page in the right conversations with the right people is the best way to ensure the mission and core purpose of your organization/family are being served.

It is critical for each employee/family member and management team to understand the risks and rewards of their behavior and decisions. As a business, what's at risk if we're not effective? What's at stake? Do we lose time? Productivity? Employees? Cohesiveness? Do we lose the magic of collaboration, the spark of creativity? Do we lose morale and motivation? Confidence? Customers? Profit? And what are the rewards? What do we gain? What, in our heart of hearts, do we want to see happen here? What would make years of hard work and dedication worth the effort?

Individuals, organizations, and families have a way of getting in their own way. The combination of being conflict-avoidant and having little, if any, training in direct, forthright communication can spell disaster even in the best-run, most technologically advanced companies, well-intending leaders, and loving families. So much has been swept under the rug and "the debt" has finally come due. Things begin to unravel. More often than not, it's a slow bleeding, and people have become used to living that way. They don't know how complacent, frenetic, miserable, and/or lucky they have become until they quit their jobs and go to work for somebody else. Or they get a new boss. Then they have an epiphany. "Wow. Not every workplace (or boss or family) is that way?"

There's no shortage of CEO's, managers, and board members who have achieved their success by sheer force and bullying. Nor is there a shortage of parents who think it's their job to "raise" their children. They get their way through intimidation, control, and domination. But once they're at the top of their industry or have taken their children as far as they can push them, bosses and parents are surprised to discover that their old ways aren't working anymore. Or how alone they are, having burned so many bridges. They reach a point of diminishing returns. Their once-effective methods of managing and parenting begin to work against them as success and confidence dwindle away.

The strong-arm behavior that's netted serious profits, earned a management title, or kept little kids in check, begins to create the opposite result. Because of my coaching client Steve's tendency to intimidate and even bully his subordinates, he had gone over the line and was almost fired on several occasions. Despite his brilliance on the job (nobody was better at crunching numbers), his board had lost faith in his management abilities. He was an incredibly astute businessman, but because of the way he was dealing with people, he had lost credibility and valuable support.

How many CEO's fall prey to their own insecurities—dictating orders to their management team that could have been functioning 100 percent more effectively, more autonomously, more collaboratively, and ultimately more productively on behalf of their fellow employees, shareholders, and customers. How many parents do the same thing with their kids? In both cases, it's a huge price to pay. Too high. The CEO's, management teams, and families who work diligently to turn things around, end up 100 percent happier and more effective. As a side benefit, their other relationships at home and work also get 100 percent better.

Getting Real—"The Point of Diminishing Returns"

The point of diminishing returns is when a flawed approach to business or personal relationships begins to have tangible negative effects. The debt incurred by the flawed approach comes due. Luckily we need not wait for things to unravel to free ourselves of the fears and insecurities that misguide us as leaders, parents, and life partners.

Real Rule #15 means that to be our best, we sometimes have to go against what we have habitually done and do something new. We have to be bigger than our fears and insecurities, get our egos out of the way, and break out of a destructive pattern. This often means getting the ball to a teammate, whether it's a co-worker, your spouse, or your child, and then cheering them on to success. But sometimes it's just us out there.

Perhaps the greatest example of this situation is professional boxing. I've been a boxing fan since my best friend's dad took us aside and taught us how to box at age ten. There's an expression in boxing: "Every fighter has a plan until he gets hit." When he struts into the ring, with the spotlight shining on him and his entourage, music blaring, crowd roaring, a boxer's ego *must* be on display—if only to dampen the fear he may feel. But once the bell rings, having a plan can literally get him killed!

Like boxers, we all have plans—until we get hit. Especially if the punch comes out of nowhere. Finding ourselves lying on the canvas, dazed, wondering what hit us, can be a defining moment of truth. It's a turning point. We can either use our brains ("What's the smartest thing for me to do right now?") or our bravado, ("I'd better do something quick to look good"). As any good trainer will tell you, doing what's necessary to gather your wits and survive the round gives you a fighting chance of getting back into the game. And possibly even winning.

We're not as special as we think. We're *more* special! But only by realizing the limits of our egos, the importance of serving/empowering others and the world beyond our blind spots, are we able to grow to new heights as people, professionals, and parents.

⟡ ⟡ ⟡

Real Action

RR#15 TAKEAWAYS

EXERCISE #1 Reading this chapter likely stirred some insights about your blind spots. Write down what you think they are.

EXERCISE #2 Next to each one, speculate about how each blind spot may have clouded your judgment and behavior.

EXERCISE #3 How might your ego be getting in the way of your effectiveness?

EXERCISE #4 Name three things you could do to turn away from arrogance and self-centeredness, and move toward more humility and service to others.

EXERCISE #5 The following questions are designed to help identify the blind spots in your life. Write your responses down on a separate piece of paper.

- Do you empower your colleagues and employees? If so, how? Could you do more to empower them?

- Do you empower your partner? If so, how? Could you do more to empower him or her?

- Do you empower your kids? If so, how? Could you do more to empower them?

- What are some practical, everyday things you could do to "pass the ball" to the other people in your life?

- If it was just you out there, like a professional boxer or skater, what do you guess would be your greatest asset? Greatest liability? Write both of them down and explain why.

Real Rule #16

LIFE CAN BE MESSY BUSINESS:
Making Peace with Chaos

This past year, I sat with the mother and father of a murdered 15-year-old as they made one of the hardest decisions of their lives. The man who raped and murdered their daughter had made a full confession. The forensic evidence eliminated any doubt: it was him.

But he had also been accused of murdering another girl, a 17-year-old, on her way home from school. And for this murder, there was no proof and no confession.

The defense struck a plea bargain. Their client was willing to plead guilty to both murders and give details of how he killed the other girl. . . if the prosecution would spare the death penalty and give him a life sentence instead.

The family had to make a choice: push to have the man who murdered their daughter killed, or forgo their vengeance in order to help another family solve the mystery of what had actually happened to their little girl.

This family appealed to a far higher principle than an eye for an eye. Despite their immeasurable pain, they chose a heart for a heart. They accepted the plea bargain, and their daughter's murderer was sentenced to life without parole.

There was a part of them—a very strong part—that wanted to see him die. That wanted to exact justice for their daughter who had been cruelly robbed of her life and her future. After what he had done, they believed, he did not deserve to live. But what won out was their compassion for another family suffering the same nightmare they were. The other family would finally get the answers they had so desperately been seeking. They'd still have to live in the horror of what happened, but they would no longer have to live in the darkness of never knowing. And the family I was working with would also have to live out their lives knowing their daughter's killer was still alive. Nonetheless, their compassion outweighed their desire for revenge.

Real Rule #16: Life Can Be Messy Business. Ends are left untied in almost all of our lives. Unfinished business can leave us with a deep sense of injustice, remorse, and heartache. Painful events can never be reversed. How we feel about them now is likely how we will always feel about them. It sucks! It always will! Things don't get better, they get different. What we do get is the ability to choose whether pain and injustice is all we will ever feel. The ability to somehow, miraculously, arise out of the ashes of tragedy and despair—and to once again feel the goodness, beauty, and majesty of life—is in us. Choosing love and compassion rather than bitterness and revenge is how we fight our way back into life. Even though the pain persists, getting back on our feet is a noble quest.

Building the Case for Letting Go

When someone commits an injustice, there needs to be accountability and consequences. I'm not denying that. The man who murdered both of those young women deserves to pay for his crimes. But the highest kind of accountability often has nothing to do with vengeance. Sometimes dying is an easy way out. And even more important, the death penalty rarely affords the victim or their family the degree of satisfaction or relief they've been expecting. I know this from experience, having watched many families before, during, and after the murder trial of someone who killed their loved one.

Families who are struggling through the grief of losing a loved one to violence spend a lot of time and energy building a case in their minds—trying to reconcile that which can never be reconciled. While the attorneys are building a legal case for the court, these men and women are building a case in their own hearts. They tell themselves that they'll feel better after the murderer or rapist is dead. That the pain of the loss will somehow be lessened.

But they're almost always disappointed. Yes, the person who committed the crime may be dead or confined in a tiny cell for life, their future obliterated. But no amount of punishment can bring back their sons or daughters. This is a matter that remains beyond the reconciliation a court of law can provide.

With all due respect to the dedicated police, district attorneys, judges, and juries who work tirelessly and often put their own lives on the line to achieve justice for victims of crime, the injustice of violent crime is never completely resolved or reconciled. If your spouse is murdered, watching the murderer be convicted doesn't change that you no longer have your loved one next to you. It may change the way you feel about what happened, and provide assurance that justice has been done, but you will likely always feel the pain of that horrible loss.

Getting Real—"No Secret Formulas or Quick Fixes"

There are no hidden stipulations for how to heal our wounds. They are what they are. All we can do is breathe in and breathe out. Hope for a better day. And perhaps, seek reconciliation on a higher level.

Some victims of crime have trouble accepting the persistent symptoms of trauma and loss. At some point, they become exasperated, "What's wrong with me? How come I can't get over this?" But the truth is that we don't get *over* some things, and vengeance isn't a cure. No amount of pain a convicted child murderer could suffer is going to change things.

Life can be messy business. Trying to "fix" that mess doesn't guarantee anything. In fact, only by acknowledging the awful, nasty, brutal truth of the mess do we begin to muster the strength and courage to get through it. Again, it is only by allowing ourselves to feel what we feel, rather than hide, deny, resist, hurry, or avoid these emotions, that we find relief, strength, and some semblance of peace.

Making a Choice

When we've suffered a loss or setback, it's almost automatic for others to try and figure out how we should move on. There's never a shortage of advice. Everybody seems to have a "take" or a "spin." After Jenna was killed, people told me, "If your daughter hadn't died, you never would have started the Jenna Druck Center, and none of this would ever have happened. Look at all the people you've helped! What a blessing."

Yes, the Jenna Druck Center has impacted the lives of many people. Instead of letting my pain become the center of the universe, I poured my love for my daughter there. I chose to honor her, and do good things in her name. To carry on her work developing young women into tomorrow's leaders. But I can't tell you how angry it makes me when people want to tie the ordeal of Jenna's death up with a neat little ribbon and a bow. Justifying my daughter's death on the basis of the good I've done is like a bad punch line on a Hallmark card: "Isn't it sweet how the universe works?" That isn't my truth. I have come to realize this is their well-meaning attempt to make sense of tragedy and keep their world somewhat orderly. But the world *isn't* orderly. It's messy.

Nothing good that could ever happen would justify my daughter's death. No matter how many wonderful things we are able to do through Jenna's center, I'd take it all back in a second for one more moment in time with Jenna.

There's no Real Rule that says life works in an orderly way. In fact Real Rule #16 says the opposite. Chaos theory is alive and well. Life makes a mess . . . a mess you can't bottle or sanitize or put a bow on, no matter how hard you try.

What you can do is accept that life is going to be life—and make the best choices you can under the circumstances. To fight your way back into life after a setback and slowly turn the pain into love. What the parents who lost their daughter did for the sake of the other grieving family was noble. It won't bring their baby back—nothing will ever do that. But they made an unselfish choice that allowed them to transcend vengeance and bring light to darkness.

We don't get to fix or undo a life loss or tragedy. We do get to honor who and what we have lost by going on to make our lives an expression of our love. We get to help ourselves survive and receive the support we need to get through the bad days. And we do get to choose a path of light, even in life's darkest, messiest moments.

Real Action

RR#16 TAKEAWAYS

Life is messy business. It's our job to summon the strength, courage, and wisdom to make peace with the chaos.

EXERCISE #1 Ask yourself the following questions, and write down the answers:

- What messes have you had to wade through in your life?

- How did they make you stronger (even if they broke your heart)?

- What life lessons did you learn along the way?

- What are some ways you could still address those losses and hurts, striving to make peace with them?

- Are there others in your life going through similar struggles to whom you could offer assistance and support?

EXERCISE #2 How could you turn the pain and loss in your life into an expression of love?

EXERCISE #3 How might you be seeking revenge or punishing yourself or others, to compensate for a loss, failure, or setback?

EXERCISE #4 What uplifting poem or daily reminder might you write on your bathroom mirror—something like "One breath at a time" or "It's okay that it's not okay"—to help you turn darkness into light? Write it down and post it.

Real Rule #17

THE VALUE OF BEING REAL:
Intimacy and Connectedness

As we learned back in Real Rule #8, listening is love. But what about our own need to be understood? What is the value of having someone bear witness to our lives as we live them?

Having a spouse, parent, and/or best friend witness your journey without judgment is one of the greatest blessings of any lifetime. It requires an intimacy of connection that is a rare and precious gift, with value too great to be quantified.

Unfortunately, seeking and building close relationships like this is no easy task. Especially when it comes to friends. We're probably introduced to literally thousands of people in our lifetimes, and only a handful ever become our truest and deepest friends, confidants, and partners. In my own life, I call such people wizards. Not wizards of Oz, but of *hearts*.

Trust me: I know.

Many years ago, I was introduced to an extraordinary man named Robert. Robert lived in Los Angeles and was a therapist. Some of his clients were not just Hollywood stars—they were Hollywood *mega*-stars. Robert has been thanked in many an Oscar acceptance speech—without anyone knowing the Academy Award winner was thanking his or her shrink! For reasons that went far beyond his ability to attract celebrity clients, Robert was a very rare and special man.

Working in psychology all of my adult life, I've also been a lifeline to a lot of people. I am blessed with heartwarming e-mails, calls, and cards from people every day, thanking me for the time I spent with them and their families—often when they didn't know how they were going to go on after a loss. When I look back on the 15 years that have passed since losing Jenna, I ask myself, "Who was a lifeline for me?" And Robert is one person who comes to mind.

Robert lives for the truth—and he lives by the Real Rules. In conversations, he always wants to get to the core of any issue. He's fearless in that sense. We don't often think about people's courage in terms of their transparency or the range of freedom or emotion they exhibit in a simple conversation, but we should. In conversation we're too often limited by poor listening, editorializing, distractions, disinterest, and elephants in the room—elements that shut us down rather than open us up.

Robert has never been interested in playing games or in playing it safe. He either wanted a deep and total friendship, or none at all. And for him, a deep friendship meant 100 percent transparency. Lucky for me, that's exactly what we've had for over 20 years.

When Jenna died, my daughter, Stefie, my wife, and I were blessed with the love and support of many friends. I will always remember and be grateful for their outpouring of generosity. Their love was unprecedented. Family and friends literally moved in with us and handled everything from the return of Jenna's body from India to the details of her memorial service. But when the service was over, the reporters left our front lawn and our friends began returning to their own lives. It was then that the shock began to wear off and the reality—that Jenna would never be coming home—set in. During those dark days, Robert was the person I turned to the most. There were times where the pain was so overwhelming that I honestly thought I was either going to die or go crazy. I would barely have the strength to pick up the phone, dial Robert's number, and say, "I'm free-falling and about to go over the edge. I just needed to hear your voice." Robert was on the other end of the line, listening, and affirming my pain. There were times when there was nothing he could say, but I always knew that he was there.

Sometimes he would cry with me. Other times he would just sit with me while I cried. The trust I had in my friend was infinite. I could talk about my worst fears and how broken I felt. I could talk about the depths of my despair. I could say anything . . . and Robert never flinched. He was always right there, exuding acceptance, kindness, and understanding.

Not only was Robert present, but he would urge me to go deeper into what I was feeling. Never once was there anything in his tone that said, "Your time is up," or "Stop, you're making me feel really uncomfortable," or "What do you expect me to say to you?" Instead, his constant reminder was, "How could you not feel that way?" If I had to define it in one word, what Robert showed me was the power and courage of *self-acceptance*.

Getting Real—"Friendship as Home"

The bird a nest, the spider a web, man friendship.

— William Blake

Not everyone is lucky enough to have this kind of friend. But everyone deserves one. We're cheating ourselves in this life if we don't open ourselves to having at least one true, deep, intimate friendship. And maybe more than one!

How Deep Friendships Are Born

In order to discover and cultivate friends like Robert, we must first *be* that kind of friend. We have to embody the honesty, kindness, understanding, trust, and loyalty we seek in others. Such extraordinary friendships often reveal themselves under one of two circumstances: great crisis, or great opportunity.

When crisis strikes, there will be people who go completely MIA—and those who show up more than we could ever imagine. I call the latter "angels." Often we don't know we have these kinds of deep and powerful friends until something bad happens. Then, suddenly, they show up big time. There are no conditions, no agendas, and they don't ask for anything in return. They're just there, giving, listening, understanding, and being present when we need them the most.

A bereaved mother named Viv recently asked me, "How do I thank all my friends who've been there every day to help my family since our son died? They've done every little thing to take care of us. They are my angels!"

"Why not have an 'angel party' in their honor?" I suggested.

Viv invited 25 of her "angels" to a beautiful dinner at her home and gave them all gifts as a way of telling them how much it meant to her for them to have shown up the way they did. Later that year, she and her husband, Mike, sponsored a fundraising dinner at the beautiful Pacific Athletic Club (PAC) where they are members. "PAC of Angels" raised over $50,000 for The Jenna Druck Center's Families Helping Families program in honor of Viv and Mike's son, Alex. Talk about paying it forward! This family not only thanked all their angels in style, they themselves became angels to the families who will now be able to get help from our center.

You don't have to go through a crisis to find the angels in your life. Sometimes angels surface in moments of great opportunity. Years ago, I was introduced by a good friend who was a well-known record company executive to a young singer-songwriter named Jewel. She and her mother were actively seeking guidance and support as they grew their nonprofit organization. Jewel had just had her first top-ten hit and was being featured on the cover of *TIME* magazine, so things were going very well for her and her mother, Lenedra. Over time, I became a trusted confidant and friend, and Jewel and her mom became ardent supporters of the Jenna Druck Center. At one point they even gave a benefit concert and mother-daughter workshop to raise money for the center. Jewel and her mom truly became "everyday angels" (Jewel's term) to the center at a time when we needed them.

Getting Real —"In the Sunshine of Life"

Thomas Jefferson once said, "But friendship is precious, not only in the shade, but in the sunshine of life." A true friend is someone who's got a shoulder to cry on during the hard times, and a high-five for when the going is good.

Sometimes it's during times of great prosperity and abundance that we really need angels. These are the friends who cheer us on and don't begrudge us our success. They're happy for us; they love and appreciate what we've done to get where we are. They will stand with us in celebration, kicking up their heels as if it were their own triumph. And in a way, it is. They are truly able to share our joy.

Real friends show up at all kinds of intersections in our lives. It might be at a point of great tragedy, but it could just as well be a moment of great triumph.

Now, you might be saying, "Well, I'm glad you've got a close friend, Ken . . . but my best friend just ran off with my wife and now I don't trust anybody." Those of us who've been hurt, betrayed, or slighted by a close friend may require time and newfound strength before we can love and trust again. But this is a risk we will eventually need to take. Some people seem to do very well by themselves but in truth we can't meet all of our own needs. Like it or not, we're social animals that need companionship. At some point we need to go outside and beyond ourselves.

Many of us have been raised in a culture that teaches us—especially men—to be staunchly independent. We're supposed to be self-reliant at all costs. Is it any wonder that "help" is the least utilized four-letter word in the male vocabulary? Yet conversations that begin with the words "I need your help" are often the most powerful and effective. So why is it so difficult for many men to ask for help without fear of looking weak or being a burden?

I can tell you what a blessing it has been to free myself from this myth of self-reliance and to be able to turn to a trusted friend like Robert. I can name a hundred dads who have lost a child and didn't have anybody to turn to until they came to a Dad's Support Group at The Jenna Druck Center. Learning to graciously accept help is a huge part of my Turning Adversity into Opportunity workshops. It's also part of being *real*.

Several years after Jenna died, Robert fell ill and required a kidney transplant. His brother stepped up and donated one of own kidneys. In the years since, Robert has continued to fight for his life. I've tried to be there for him in much the same way that he's been there for me. Thankfully, he is doing better and even met a wonderful woman with whom he shares his days and his life's work. I love Robert dearly as a brother. Our friendship is one of the great blessings of my life.

I hope you will consider making even more room in your life for and/or celebrating the Wizards of Hearts in your life.

Real Action

RR#17 TAKEAWAYS

True friends don't come along every day. That's why it's important to continue to cultivate the friendships you've built over the years. Think of it as putting money into a bank—the more you put in, the more there is to withdraw when you need it. As Ralph Waldo Emerson said, "The only way to have a friend is to be one."

EXERCISE #1 Are you a good friend? You might consider taking the Friend Report Card on my website. See how you fare and where there's room for improvement.

EXERCISE #2 Try one or more of the following to let your friends know how special they are to you:

- Host an angel party to say "thanks" to all those who have been there for you.

- Take a close friend out to a nice meal and tell them what their friendship means to you.

- Make more time for intimate conversations with the friends that really mean something to you.

- Write a friend a letter highlighting five things you really like, respect, and admire about them. Or, write about what you are grateful to them for.

- Offer specific forms of assistance—such as cooking a meal or watching their kids—to a friend who is going through a particularly hard time.

Real Rule #18

LOSING IT IS FINDING IT:
Don't Shoot the Messenger (of Emotions)

A few months ago, I was attending the annual Young Women's Spirit of Leadership Conference hosted by The Jenna Druck Center. What I didn't know was that our Program Director, Leanne, and her staff had planned a surprise memorial to commemorate the 15th anniversary of Jenna's death.

And so, on March 27, the day of the conference, they showed a beautiful film of Jenna. Seeing her alive and smiling always takes my breath away. A very talented and loving singer-songwriter named Stephanie Johnson performed songs she had written for the occasion. And finally, all 400 girls at the conference released balloons into the blue sky to which they had attached special messages to Jenna. As they let go of their balloons, my earth daughter, Stefie, who volunteers for The Jenna Druck Center's Families Helping Families and Spirit of Leadership programs, placed her hand softly on my shoulder. And then came the tears.

I'm often asked to be strong for the people who are suffering tremendous loss and grief in their lives. But in that moment, I had permission to feel the deep sorrow of my own loss.

Like most guys, I'd grown up with the idea that any display of emotion (other than anger) demoted you to "lesser man" status on the "Male Scale." This was the ethic that many of the men in my generation grew up with. It was basic training for being a man.

Taught by our fathers and grandfathers to "be strong," and "keep it together," "losing it" was the ultimate humiliation. It was a sure sign of weakness. Real men, we believed, didn't fall apart. They were never reduced to tears, because big boys don't cry.

Unfortunately, we were presented with a very unreal and constricted model of what it means to be a man. Or a human being.

It's been a lifelong goal of mine, as a man and as a teacher, to be able to let down, show emotion, and let tears fall where they will without feeling like I'm any lesser or weaker of a man. A fundamental part of my mental health and the central theme of my first book, *The Secrets Men Keep*, is fighting for the freedom and confidence to be myself. To be real and authentic, not some watered-down version of who I really am. Of course, even in today's society, that's easier said than done. There is so much fear—fear of being judged, fear of being ridiculed, fear of losing control and respect.

Getting Real —"When Losers Win"

In our society, the idea of losing almost always has a negative connotation. We talk about losing our jobs and losing our cool. Nobody wants to be labeled a "loser." But the ancient root of this losing is the Latin *luere,* meaning "to atone for." Atonement comes from a Middle English root meaning "to become reconciled." Sometimes only by "losing it" are we able to access the inner strength to reconcile the losses and disappointments in our lives

Throughout the anniversary event, I'd been trying to hold it together. Trying to be strong for the 400 girls at the conference, our staff, and the foundation I created in Jenna's honor. But all it took was Stefie's hand on my shoulder for me to let down my guard and allow myself to really miss her sister.

I can't break down in front of all these girls, I thought. *It would be too upsetting to them.* And in almost the same instant, I realized: *I'm not losing it. I've found it!* I had tapped into my wellspring of sorrow about losing Jenna and my love for both of my daughters. I allowed the tears to fall.

In that moment, I rediscovered the freedom to show how much I love and miss Jenna. And how grateful I was to have Stefie right there with me. Far from scaring the girls, the tears that ran down my cheek elicited their compassion. Within seconds, I had over ten hands on my shoulders, besides Stefie's. The girls started coming up, patting me on the shoulder, and hugging me. Many of them don't have fathers present in their lives. But reaching out to me, they could experience—some for the first time—father-daughter love.

In that moment, as the balloons lifted softly into a cloudless, blue sky, I felt surrounded by daughterly love. The true power of Real Rule #18 is that sometimes just when we think we're "losing it," we're actually finding the thing we've been looking for.

Big Boys Do Cry

It's not easy being a guy. Just because we act tough or unfazed doesn't mean we're not hurting, in very deep and profound ways.

Like any human being, men experience tragedy and loss. The difference is in how we *deal* with it. Whether we've lost our job or someone dear to us, we try to hold it together. Sadly, this posturing has not changed much over the years, in the same way that young girls still equate physical beauty with self-worth. We fight off the tears because we're afraid that crying makes us look weak. But regardless as to whether we manage to keep the tears at bay, we're still crying on the inside. Yes, as men we learn how to cry on the inside. And we do it all the time, silently and secretly. It's one of the secrets that men still keep. We may appear calloused and unfeeling, but we are actually extremely sensitive. It's just that we've been taught to keep those "soft" feelings private.

What is it we're so afraid of? Actually, it's several things. First, we're grappling with the fear of being judged. And second, we're afraid of losing face or status. Meyer Friedman, the man who first coined type-A behavior and one of my mentors, referred to this as "status insecurity."

As men, we work hard to achieve respect and stature. And to get it, we often feel the need to conform to the cultural ideal of what it means to be a man. It's the strong, tough men who are celebrated—they're the cowboys in the old Westerns, or the superheroes who get all the glory (and the pretty girls). The message is that a real man wins the respect and admiration of others by being tough—definitely not by crying.

Remember that scene in *Field of Dreams* where a father and son play catch? That scene always has a powerful effect on men, and it certainly had a powerful effect on me. The image of a little boy and his dad brings back images of the child we all used to be—and the father we all longed for.

Ask any man about his relationship with his dad, and if he's honest with you and with himself, he's apt to get tearful. For nearly ten years, I traveled the world giving workshops for men and asking that exact question. The Alive and Male workshops would start with 35 men breaking into small groups. Everybody would share the story of what happened in their relationship with their dads. No matter where I went in the world, every single man—whether they were executives or a bunch of pub crawlers from Sydney, Australia—had tears.

Most men told stories about their emotionally unavailable and physically absent fathers, and how they'd spent their whole lives secretly yearning for love and validation from their dads (or "dad substitutes," like coaches and bosses). Occasionally somebody would have had an amazing dad—the dad everybody else wanted—who taught them what it really meant to be a human being, not just a man, and how this had set the tone for their entire life. Either way, these grown men had tears welling up in their eyes. They were grieving for those lost fathers, and for themselves as sons, too. They cried for the little boys who, in the absence of real, flesh-and-blood examples of what it means to be a man, had to find role models in celebrities like John Wayne, James Bond, Mickey Mantle, and Michael Jordan.

Getting Real —"A Man's Man"

Despite shifting gender roles, the culture of pseudo-masculinity is still alive and well. And while many traits of a traditional "man's man" are innocuous and even admirable, men who are unable to show up emotionally in a relationship ultimately suffer—as do their partners, children, co-workers, and friends.

In the rush to grow up and be a man, we abandon the boy in us who wanted and needed love and validation, but was forced to "be a man!" Society was, and is, unforgiving. We've been encouraged to forget that little boy—to bury him down deep in our psyches because he poses a threat. He might embarrass us, expose our "soft" vulnerable side, or get us demoted in status on the "Male Scale." It's much the same reason we push our mothers away when we hit adolescence—for fear we'll be labeled a "mama's boy." In so many ways we are prisoners of status insecurity.

But that little boy is not lost forever; he's just lost to us. We've posed and postured to become a caricature of a man who is "all grown up." Who's got it all together. But there are still some very young parts in all of us—and I use the word "young" deliberately—that have never learned that it's okay to be human. And when we least expect it, these young parts of us show up and surprise us. We might be in a movie theater, at a funeral, reading aloud to our children, or at a wedding when emotions well up inside us and spill over. Something gives way, and we can no longer deny them.

When it happens, we often try to cover up our emotions as quickly as possible. This happens even when the feeling is one of genuine affection or concern. Think back to the characters Danny Zuko and Kenickie in the classic 1970s movie *Grease*. When Zuko narrowly escapes death, these bosom buddies forget about being tough guys for a split second and hug each other . . . and then just as quickly, they're reaching for their combs to reclaim their cool. There's an immediate knee-jerk reaction when we've mistakenly exposed a young, vulnerable part of us. We showed how much we really cared—and now we have to cover it up.

Most of this is as true today as it was in the 1980s, when I wrote a book on this subject and traveled the world being interviewed on TV and radio, giving workshops and presenting keynote speeches about the secrets men keep. Some things are so deeply and intractably embedded in our society, they change slowly or defy change altogether.

But you need not. Understanding the young, unsure parts of yourself and embracing them sets you free. Real men do cry, and it's not only okay. It's *good* for you.

When we cry, our brain releases endorphins that pump feel-good chemicals into our bodies and actually balance our moods. Sighing has the same effect. That's why in yoga, they teach you to breathe and sigh. Emitting vibrational sounds—like a simple "om"—can also calm the body and relax the mind.

Crying is not always the best and only thing to do. Nor is it always appropriate. And feelings do not come with a license to always express them. I don't want my airline pilot or brain surgeon breaking down on the job. My point is simply that it's not always the wrong thing to do. At the right time and in the right place, it's incredibly freeing to be able to express the sorrow or exuberance we feel with no shame, apology, or defense. What a powerful and authentic expression of your humanity—of what it means to be a flesh and blood human. As the old saying goes, "People respect you for your image, but they love you for your vulnerability."

When we allow ourselves to let down our guard and tap into the core of our humanity, we're not losing it. We're *finding it*, even if "it" has lain dormant beneath our tough façade for many years. Sure, some of the people in our lives might be uncomfortable as we become more real and open—and they may judge us. But they also may feel as though they finally have access to "the real us," and draw even closer. The fact that we are no longer posing, posturing, and inwardly judging ourselves to be less of a man, or a woman, is what sets us free.

This newfound freedom, a recurring theme in this book, connects us in a deeper, more meaningful and satisfying way to ourselves, our lives, and to others. When we insist on the real thing, we bring out the very best in ourselves and those around us.

Real Action

<u>RR#18 TAKEAWAYS</u>

Don't shoot the messenger of emotions—they're fundamental to your healing process. When you pick up sorrow, despair, or fear on your radar screen, it may help to remind yourself that:

- It's okay to show real emotion, and to cry.

- It's okay to be vulnerable and tell the truth about how you feel—it doesn't mean you're weak.

- It's okay to "lose it." You haven't really lost anything, you've only gained a healthy outlet for bottled up emotions.

EXERCISE #1 As a self-assessment exercise, rate yourself from 1 to 10 with "Free to Feel" being a 10 and "Emotionally Shut Down" being a 1.

EXERCISE #2 Do a risk assessment on your approach to dealing with your emotions. Describe several situations in which you might be shooting the messenger by hiding, denying, or repressing your emotions. Next to each, complete the sentences "What's at risk if I share this feeling is___" and "What's at risk if I don't is ___."

EXERCISE #3 How does the way you manage your emotions help you in the world? How might it hurt you?

EXERCISE #4 Are certain emotions more acceptable in your culture? Or for your gender? Which ones? Which ones are prohibited?

Real Rule #19

AIN'T NO FAIRY GODMOTHER:
The Courage to Move Forward

A good friend of mine, a psychologist, recently married a successful trial attorney. It was a second marriage for both of them. When I asked how things were going, he told me, "We've been fighting a lot but it's actually very funny. She fights like an attorney, and I fight like a shrink!"

My friend's wife was, like any good lawyer, fierce and adversarial. She held a hard line. My friend, on the other hand, was all about sharing feelings and making peace. A nice guy. He functioned under the basic assumption that everything could be worked out if everyone just acted nice.

Unfortunately, he found out that's not always the case. There are times when being nice just doesn't cut it. Sometimes, we need to draw a line in the sand. Sooner or later, life challenges each of us to speak up for what we believe in. And that's what my buddy had to learn how to do. Once he got clear and made a stand for what he wanted, things began to "magically" get better. He and his wife developed a newfound respect, confidence in their ability to talk things out, and clarity about how the other one really felt. With things out on the table, some of the tension lifted and the fire that was there when they met was rekindled.

There's a warrior within all of us—a fierce, strong part that knows how to set hard boundaries. This side of us is clear, forceful, courageous, and intentional, but it can also be peaceful. It does not necessarily allow disagreements to escalate into an argument or violence. A warrior need never be a bully.

Dan Millman's landmark book, *Way of The Peaceful Warrior*, was in Jenna's backpack at the time of her death. Judging from the pages that were tagged with stickies, Jenna would probably say that there is a peaceful warrior within all of us. We can call upon that part of ourselves for great courage in moments of truth.

Getting Real—"Strength of Heart"

A person with strength of heart knows their own boundaries, and they respect the boundaries of others. They're willing to take a conversation wherever it needs to go without using scare tactics, power plays, or insults. They stand up for themselves, the other person, and the relationship.

There are times in all of our lives when we discover that we may have inadvertently become a doormat—perhaps in the context of a romantic relationship or a job. We were being thrown under the bus, and may not have even realized it. Perhaps there was too much at risk and we were afraid to take a stand. We didn't want to rock the boat—so we stuck our head in the sand. Committed to keeping the peace at all costs, we paid dearly by absorbing unnecessary, undeserved hardship and even abuse.

There's nothing wrong with compromise, and a willingness to sacrifice is often the key to successful relationships. But when we abuse ourselves or enable others in their abusive behavior, we are putting ourselves and the people we love at risk. Still, finding the strength to stand up to what's happening by setting a hard boundary with an indelible edge is not always easy.

Drawing a line in the sand means risking the consequences. You are likely to get your hands dirty. Setting boundaries calls out important issues. It may even take the relationship itself to task—and very possibly destabilize it. But having strength of heart means standing up for yourself and what really matters. We all face these critical choice points. They define our character and integrity.

Every serious relationship passes through moments of truth. A husband and wife might decide whether they're willing to do what is necessary to have their marriage work. Maybe one partner agrees to stop overspending, curb flirtatious behavior, or get out of a bad job. Perhaps a lifelong workaholic cuts back his hours to make time for his special-needs son, while an executive rededicates herself to addressing a health problem that's beginning to impinge on her family, her company, and her health.

One of my neighbors has a teenage son who is in dire trouble with drugs. For years his father wouldn't own up to the problem, even though he knew his boy was playing with fire. Finally, after his son was arrested with a car full of nonprescription drugs, he had to admit that they had a serious problem. His denial had been shattered for the moment. Would he put his head back in the sand? Thankfully not. It took courage, conviction, and strength of heart to face his son's problem head-on. He weathered the legal consequences, got his son the help he needed, and threw himself 100 percent into "Family Week" at the 30-day treatment facility where his son had been admitted.

In these pivotal moments, we are asked to transcend who we've been up to that point. We step out of the shadow of avoidance, denial, intimidation, and fear. We admit where we've allowed or enabled a dangerous situation, and put ourselves on the line. Then we rise to the challenge—and make a change.

These are the moments when we become our own hero. We drop all of the excuses, rationalizations, justifications, and outright BS we've been feeding ourselves for not taking action. Instead, we tap into a wellspring of strength and courage we may never before have called upon. You may be on the verge of such a decision. If so, stop looking around for excuses and look in the mirror. You may be just the hero you've been waiting for.

The Real Magic

We all harbor a secret hope that the tough situations in our lives will magically get better. We yearn, hope, and pray for something to change, and sometimes we get so caught up in wishful thinking that we procrastinate taking action ourselves. We're busy or overwhelmed, or we're so frantically hoping and praying for a miracle that we fail to recognize Real Rule #19: Ain't No Fairy Godmother.

If you wait for someone else (Mom, Dad, God, your spouse, doctor, boss, or minister) to come and save you, you'll likely be waiting forever. The responsibility is on you to put your life in order and get it on a better track. There are no fairy godmothers. It's up to you to make changes in your life, even the ones that appear impossible. ("The impossible just takes a little longer" a very successful CEO once told me.)

Making these changes may be the scariest thing you've ever done. Imagine a woman sitting at the police station with two black eyes. The officers are saying, "Ma'am, we need you to press charges." And she responds, "But he's such a good man . . . and I love him."

She's not only scared of her husband's wrath; she's scared of inducing an irreversible crisis in her family. Yes, her spouse may have battered her; yes, he may be doing drugs and inviting dangerous people into their home; yes, he's surely putting their children at risk on a daily basis. But by turning him in, she fears she will be destabilizing their lives in an even more drastic way. She's faced with going back to the same situation, praying and hoping that it won't unravel again, or making a bold change that will affect every aspect of her (and her family's) life. As the saying goes, "The devil you know is better than the one you don't."

Being the whistle-blower comes with a cost. Whether the subject is domestic abuse, illegal business practices in your corporation, or your very own BS, blowing the whistle will shake up your world. To be willing to do this, you must have faith. By facing a bad situation and saying "enough!" you're actually laying the foundation for a better future.

When called to make a change in our lives, we often go through a gestation period. Getting a divorce, making a job change, stopping drinking, losing weight, leaving an abusive relationship—all of these are bold acts that take time and great dedication. You are disengaging from the life you had and reconfiguring parts of your existence. It could be weeks, months, or years until things level out—and that's okay. These changes take as long as they take, unfolding in their own unique way. As I have said to myself so many times—because it is worth repeating— each of us is a "work in progress." But we must believe that somehow, some way, our dedication and commitment to opening a new chapter will pay off.

If you're considering making a significant change, here are some steps you can take. First, form a clear picture in your mind and heart of the desired outcome (i.e., what it's all going to look and feel like when things do change). This is your anchor. My dear friend, best-selling author and "Spiritual Entrepreneur" John Assaraf, teaches people how to assemble Dream Boards from magazine clippings, drawings, and anything else that depicts their dreams for the future. Making such a board helps you set your sights on a vision. Then you need only have faith in yourself until you can say with conviction, "I can do this!"

Step two is to get real with yourself about what's *been* going on. Take ownership and responsibility for where you are right now and how you got there. Shortcomings, procrastination, excuses and all. Make an honest admission about the fears, insecurities, defense mechanisms, and patterns that have been holding you back from where you want to be and say, "This is what I did!"

The third step is to be kind and even merciful—with yourself. Instead of beating yourself up for the past, show that you truly understand why, up until now, this was your way of living, surviving, and making sense of your world. You did the best you could at the time. And today is a new day. Solidify your faith in your ability to change over time. It's about saying: "What I've been doing doesn't give me the results I want and deserve." If you've been playing the victim, for example, you might say, "Victim mentality has been a stopgap solution in my life, but it's not working anymore."

The fourth step is to break your plan into small steps on a critical path to reaching your goal. Clarify your blueprint for change by listing everything you need to do to be successful. Also, list all the ways you could sabotage yourself along the way.

And finally, take a bold step forward. This means taking action! Implement step one of the game plan.

This kind of a plan is the *real* magic. Take responsibility and own up to the past. Rededicate yourself to a better life, set your sights on a goal, and reassure yourself about all the good that is going to come from making this journey.

It's the voice of confidence that we want to tap into here, not a voice of fear, judgment, and condemnation. This is the voice that has imagined a better future for you and a higher expression of who you are in your family, your job, and your community. And this is the spirit in which we will continue to courageously face up to what isn't working and do everything we can to change it. It's time to remove whatever obstacles may be standing between you and a far more fulfilling future. It's time for courage, faith, and action.

Forming Your Personal Advisory Board

It's sometimes difficult to see the ways we interfere with our own success. After all, it can be daunting to look at ourselves honestly.

I encourage my coaching clients to form a Personal Advisory Board (PAB) for this exact reason. The PAB usually consists of four to five trusted friends, knowledgeable business associates, and your partner or spouse—the people who are closest to you and who know you the best. When asked to facilitate a PAB meeting, I instruct the invited participants to provide honest, direct feedback about how my clients could be more effective in their lives.

Getting Real—"A Personal Advisory Board"

A PAB works best when it's composed of four or five people you trust and respect, people who know you well. Meeting guidelines should be clearly established at the beginning in regard to things like best meeting practices, desired outcome, feedback sought, time frame, confidentiality, recording of notes, and action items and rules of engagement.

Assembling a personal board of advisors is a bold way to face into our most stubborn challenges, prepare for a new season of life, and move forward. With the help of a hand-selected group of friends and advisors who genuinely care, we address the issues and challenges that have been, or could potentially be, holding us back.

I've been facilitating PAB meetings with my coaching clients for more than 25 years. Subjects have ranged from how to manage the family business to telling the people in your inner circle that you are dying. It's difficult to imagine how intimate and powerful these meetings are. How intently the advisors listen to my client and offer their input. How direct and concrete, practical and spiritual these meetings are. And how significantly clients are impacted by what happens, especially when they follow through with their agreements.

As a result of things like coaching and PAB meetings, my clients are able to refocus on the things that are truly the priorities in their lives. They confront behaviors that inhibit progress, such as blind spots, egotistical leadership, and close-mindedness. What we have at the end of the meeting is a very powerful, clear statement: "Here is exactly what I want and what I need to do to get the results I desire."

Each of us possesses the ability to make this life more of what we want it to be. We can all ask for help pushing forward when we need it. The question is: Are we committed enough to make it happen?

Commitment means putting our values, our passions, and our love on the line. If we can do all three, we'll be able to look in the mirror one day and say, "I truly gave it my best. I gave this life my best shot. I faced into those things that were difficult, I fought hard for what I wanted, and I did the best I could."

So if you want to meet a determined man or woman . . . look with gentle eyes in the mirror. It's on you to make your life come true. It's happening on your watch! Take a deep breath, clear your mind, "place your fears on the tip of your sword" (to quote an old warrior brother of mine), and go for it!

Real Action

<u>RR#19 TAKEAWAYS</u>

Being your own hero means finding the courage to move forward through trials and difficult times. Remember the five steps:

1. Form a picture in your mind of the desired outcome.

2. Take inventory of your current situation, and accept responsibility where needed without giving way to feelings of shame and blame.

3. Make an honest admission about the fears, insecurities, defense mechanisms, and patterns that may have gotten you into the situation. Be kind and merciful to yourself. Instead of denigrating yourself, reflect on how this has been a functioning means of survival up until now.

4. Solidify your faith and commitment to a better way, and a plan to work toward it. Break it down into small practical steps.

5. Take action! Take a bold step forward, make mid-course adjustments when necessary, and prepare for the changes that may follow.

You're worth it! And so will be the effort you put into it.

EXERCISE #1 Name five people you would have on your Personal Advisory Board. What is the most important subject they could help you tackle? What would hold you back from calling together your PAB and scheduling a Saturday morning to get their help?

EXERCISE #2 Name three things you could do to become your own hero.

Real Rule #20

YOU HAVE FAR LESS AND FAR MORE POWER THAN YOU KNOW: Balancing Control with Surrender

There's a renowned tae kwon do master in California—one of the best in the business—who told me about a night he was driving home from the dojo when a Jeep full of young men pulled up beside him at a red light. They started taunting him for being Asian, throwing all sorts of barbs and insults in his direction.

Now, this man is one of the preeminent masters of tae kwon do in the Western world. He could kill someone before they even had time to take a breath. He's not the guy you want to mess with. But tae kwon do is all about control, and so he didn't respond to the taunting. Instead, the master kept his eyes straight ahead and ignored them.

As soon as the light turned green, the driver of the Jeep slammed his foot down on the accelerator . . . and smashed full-speed into the car ahead.

The master looked over at them as he passed by and said simply, "Good job!"

Sometimes surrendering power, or resisting the invitation into a power struggle, is the most powerful thing we can do.

One of the fundamental tenets of Alcoholics Anonymous, a wise and powerful self-help program for alcoholics and addicts that I've come to admire and refer people to over the years, is that we're all powerless. Rather than limiting us, admitting such a sense of powerlessness actually sets us free. There are some things in life that you just can't handle, and you no longer have to. There's no defeat. No dishonor. No chickening out—far from it. Surrender simply means refusing to play when there can be no winners.

We have the power to create and re-create, define and design our lives. We have endless opportunities for change, transformation, and the realization of greater possibilities. Paradoxically, we are also powerless. We face significant limitations in the world and within ourselves that are difficult—if not impossible—to overcome. But there are, of course, steps we can (and must) take to protect ourselves; to keep ourselves, families, communities, and environment safe and healthy.

Real Rule #20: you have far less power than you know, and infinitely more than you could ever imagine. This Real Rule is a little tricky but it can set you free. The key is in mastering the art of self-empowerment.

Taking a Stand

Jackie is a very successful 37-year-old HR specialist whose company I've been working with for several years. She recently asked to meet with me for some personal coaching about a situation involving her husband, Ray, a successful scientist. Turns out that Ray is also a brilliant tactician of mind control and guilt who is (and has been) manipulating his wife for years. Ray knows how to play Jackie like a harp and preys upon her insecurities and self-doubts. This has been driving her crazy, and now it's driving her away.

At first Jackie didn't really understand why she was falling out of love with her husband and thinking about leaving him. Toward the end of our meeting, however, she began to see the ways in which he had been manipulating her, and how she had allowed him to. She began to appreciate how prone to guilt she had become. Our coaching session ended with Jackie taking home a new game plan. She would talk with her husband about what had been happening and continue to work on reducing her guilt.

When I saw Jackie a month later, she told me things had not been going well and that she had told her husband she was seriously considering a divorce. Unfortunately, Ray was continuing to use the same mind games—this time to make it very difficult for her to leave him. With their divorce now imminent, he's taunting and harassing her. Ray is a master at saying just the right things to Jackie to induce feelings of guilt, blame, fear, and shame in her. He then apologizes and reverts back to being the "great guy" who offers her the world if she would just agree not to leave him. The good news is that she is finally beginning to understand what he's doing—how she has let herself be controlled—and to put a stop to it.

Family is the most important thing for Jackie. Because Ray knows what meaning family has for her, he preys upon her sense of loyalty and refers to her leaving as a "betrayal." In the past, she would do anything to placate a bad situation, avoiding conflict at all costs. For years, she deferred to Ray, all because she feared his response.

It has been incredibly difficult for Jackie to learn how to say to Ray, "You can't do this to me anymore. You can't be accusatory and mean-spirited, and then come back being sweet and loving and apologetic, only to do it all over again. And you can't blame me for the failure in our relationship. I'm not doing this anymore. I'm done!"

Getting Real—"The Rules of Negotiation"

Sometimes in the middle of a negotiation, whether it's business-related or a conversation with our spouse, things can get pretty intense. No matter the situation, it is always within your power to pause the negotiation and ask for a few minutes to gather your thoughts and clear your head. We can get so caught up playing defense that we forget we're allowed to take a brief "time-out" to get honest with ourselves about what we really want.

Jackie's blind spot has been her refusal (and/or inability) to see how susceptible she is. It's been hard for her to accept that a lot of people—her husband most of all—prey upon her guilt and her willingness to take responsibility and blame for other people's upsets and unhappiness. She has, until now, allowed herself to feel powerless and defenseless against her own guilt. Her friends can sit there until they are blue in the face telling her not to feel responsible for other people's crap, but it has never sunk in. Only by admitting her own powerlessness can she begin to free herself from her husband's grasp and minimize the adverse effects fear has had on her life.

It's true that Jackie is powerless. And yet, in other ways, she is powerful beyond measure. She recently played me a last ditch voice mail she'd received from Ray saying, "I want to meet with you later tonight. You have to do this for me, Jackie!" In the past, being the peacemaker and pleaser, she would have acquiesced without question. Since she'd threatened to leave him, he had been using these meetings to verbally beat her up. He'd insist she was certifiably crazy to leave him; that she was "misguided" and that she had "abandoned" him and their family.

But this time, she was ready for a change. She calmly asked, "Tell me why you want to meet with me. I need to know before I agree to anything."

To her amazement, he let it go. All he said was, "Never mind," and hung up.

She was stunned. She couldn't believe she'd done it. "Usually when he calls asking to meet up," she admitted, "I say yes. I already feel guilty enough about leaving him. So he snaps his fingers and I go." She gave me a triumphant smile and a fist bump. "Not this time, Ken."

Jackie realized she had the power to protect herself from her husband's abuse by setting clear boundaries. She had taken a stand. It would take practice and some getting used to, but the alternative—letting herself get run over—was no longer acceptable. She was powerless *and* powerful—at the same time.

You Got the Power . . .

Many of us are unaware of the power we possess. And it's not just women like Jackie who are searching for the strength to change a bad situation—it's men as well. Men like former President Ronald Reagan.

In *President Reagan: The Role of A Lifetime*, journalist and author Lou Cannon recounts how in 1982, the president was frustrated with Menachem Begin, the Prime Minister of Israel, for expanding the war in Lebanon. Reagan told his advisors, "I'm really unhappy about this," to which one replied, "Why don't you pick up the phone and call him."

So Reagan did. He called Begin and told him he didn't like what was going on.

An hour later, the Oval Office received satellite reports that the shooting in Israel had moved in another direction. President Reagan looked at his advisors and said, "I didn't know I could do that!"

The paradox hidden inside Real Rule #20 is that we have infinitely more power than we could ever imagine. This is true whether you're the President of the United States or a man or woman searching for the strength to break free of an abusive relationship. At the same time that we're completely powerless, we also have far more power than we think.

President Reagan realized he had the power to stop something happening thousands of miles away simply by saying, "That's not acceptable to me." But power can manifest itself in smaller proclamations. "I don't have to live this way" is just as potent.

Paradoxically, we often arrive at that proclamation by first admitting that we feel powerless. But we might also arrive at it through a sense of outrage and humiliation. Someone has finally crossed the line and we can't be pushed any further. We're furious. "Enough!" we declare. Hitting the wall is what it takes. We realize we have to do something; that now is the time.

Getting Real—"Power Over Self"

He is most powerful who has power over himself. — Seneca

Now Let It Go

There are many things in our lives over which we have no control, as we have seen throughout this book. We can try to protect ourselves all day long, but in the end we are still powerless to prevent the setbacks we all suffer as a part of life. So we must learn to surrender to that which is bigger than us.

One of my favorite stories about surrender is that of a Buddhist teacher whose only son died suddenly. The teacher left his monastery for several months to be with his family, and when he came back, he was still very distraught. His students gathered around him and one commented, "Master, you have deep rings around your eyes and the joy is gone from your face. You taught us that all of life is but an illusion! And yet you look so very broken."

The teacher looked back at his young students, paused, and said, "Yes. Life *is* an illusion. But children are the greatest illusion of all."

There are some things we cannot transcend, choiceless moments of pain and loss when philosophy, psychology, and even religion are useless. In these moments, abstraction and doctrine cannot speak to or satisfy the wounds of the heart. The depth of our love—whether for our family, friends, or the organization we've poured our soul into—can break open our hearts. And when it does, it's okay to remember that our pain is choiceless. No matter what we've done to prepare, or how "positive" we are about the glass being half full, sorrow will have its way with us.

There are literally hundreds of "think positive" books and websites with "It's your choice to be happy!" as their central theme. The thought of looking into the eyes of a bereaved parent whose five-year-old daughter just died and saying, "Remember: It's your choice to be happy!" hurts my heart. Ninety percent of the time, these books are right. We *do* have a choice. And we should do everything in our power to make it a good one. But 10 percent of the time, it's an insult to people's intelligence and humanity to tell them that it's their choice to be happy or to have a nice day when their heart is broken and their dreams of the future have been altered forever.

In any given moment, there are countless people across our beautiful planet who are suffering terribly. In a living hell, they have absolutely no power to change their situation. But *we* have the power to do something. Visionary leaders like Mother Teresa, Gandhi, and Martin Luther King, Jr. who commit their lives to ending poverty, violence, hunger, disease, pollution, hatred, brutality, and slavery—and who champion peace, justice, and human rights—are living testimony to what is possible. Meanwhile, those who suffer will continue to summon whatever strength and resources they can to carry on through the grief, heartache, and injustices they endure.

We have the power to heal. To rise out of the ashes of despair. To live and fight another day. To prevail over even the greatest periods of turmoil in our lives, as my good friend, Susan did. Susan's husband of 32 years was caught in a terrible scandal last year and is now serving time. He is also being sued for a large sum of money. Needless to say, this has turned Susan's life (and heart) inside out. She has lost her husband and is probably going to lose her home and a good part of their life savings.

Several months ago, Susan decided to move in with her daughter a few towns away and to legally separate from her husband. This has angered her children, who still do not know the full extent of their father's wrongdoings and cannot understand why Susan is "abandoning him." Most days, she fluctuates between feeling terribly guilty, furiously angry, and just sad.

Living in her daughter's small guest house gave Susan some measure of peace. The only friend with whom she's stayed in touch bought her a small peach tree. There was something about putting her fingers into the soil and planting that tree that made her feel good for the first time in many months—and she decided to put in a small garden. Watering and taking care of her plants every day became a refuge from the world. Her garden was a source of peace, hope, new life, and a new season.

In his classic work *Candide*, Voltaire wrote, *"Il faut cultiver son jardin"*—"It's necessary to cultivate your garden." If we ever find ourselves in a winter of turmoil, like Susan, perhaps our spring can start somewhere unexpected, like the backyard.

Our most horrific suffering and losses, as my dear Uncle Irv (whose wife was a Holocaust survivor) reminded me in a letter sent shortly after Jenna's death, is the darkness we must summon the strength to overcome. We can lift ourselves up out of even the greatest despair. And help others do the same. Yes, we are powerless, white flags flapping in the turbulent winds of life . . . *and* we are powerful, beyond measure and imagination.

Real Action

RR#20 TAKEAWAYS

Though we are powerless when faced with the often-overwhelming challenges life puts in our paths, there are many things over which we do have control. Ironically, sometimes we can only access this hidden reserve of power when we admit our own powerlessness.

Remember that:

- You have the power to define and design your life, and to set your terms.

- Most of us can name a situation, work- or relationship-related, in which we have felt relatively powerless. Acknowledging and accepting this actually helps us regain power in our lives and make needed changes.

- You have the power to re-create your personal journey, choosing a healthy, whole alternative. It's never too late to tap the strength and get the help you need to change course.

EXERCISE #1 List a few of the opportunities for change and transformation that currently exist in your life.

EXERCISE #2 If you have not chosen a "cause" worthy of your time and support—one that actively reduces or alleviates the suffering of others—which ones would you consider getting involved with? Consider contacting them for more information.

Real Rule #21

"HOME FREE" IS A BILL OF GOODS:
Stop Waiting for Perfect

How many of us construct our worlds around the notion that some-day, somehow, we'll be "home free"? I think we all do it! We're waiting for the moment when everything's going to be perfect. The moment when we can check off all the items on our to-do list and the chaos of life will finally clear, like clouds moving across the sky. The stress of life's problems will be gone and we'll be flooded with an overwhelming sense of peace. All will be well.

My favorite cartoon shows a man and woman standing over a mail-box reading a letter. "It's a letter of approval from everyone I've ever known for everything I've ever done," the man exclaims with a gleeful smile.

Freedom is one of the most natural human longings—we yearn for peace, for life to come to a rest. Maybe we have three kids and find ourselves praying for a time when we won't have to be worrying about school, carpooling, after-school activities, runny noses, and the seem-ingly endless stream of demands that raising kids puts on us. We'll have earned it, won't we? Or maybe we've slaved away at the same job for 40 years, working for the same impossible boss for basically the same pay.

"If I can just get to retirement," we tell ourselves, "I'll be home free. Then I'll start really living."

But that's not the way it works, is it? Things like retirement, divorce, and having your kids turn 18 come with their own set of challenges. Adult children can be dependent well into their 30s. Retirement can often be radically different than what we expected. It can usher in unexpected feelings of emptiness and self-doubt because we're no longer doing all the things that gave us a sense of identity or purpose. Instead of "the boss," we become simply, "Joe." Or maybe we're confronted by more "face time" in a marriage than we've had in decades. We're not used to spending so much time with our husband, and we end up feeling like our boundaries have been invaded. Suddenly there's an entirely new challenge: how to coexist with our spouse over the course of an entire day—and survive.

One of my clients, a financial planner, jokes about "the three Ds" that follow retirement: divorce, depression, and death. It's tongue-in-cheek, of course, but sadly there's some truth to it. Many men and women forget to plan for or ease into such a major shift and the sudden loss of identity takes them by unwelcome surprise.

It's not just retirement. It could be any milestone you've set for yourself in the back of your mind—selling the company, getting married, getting divorced, turning 45, making your first million, moving to a new city. We think that once we've reached that milestone, acquired that one status symbol, achieved a certain measure of wealth, left a bad situation, or checked off the final item on our bucket list, we'd be home free. Done! If we can just get there and cross that imaginary finish line, then our happiness, identity, need for approval, and sense of security will be sealed forever. And then, to our surprise, the day arrives . . . and we're surprised to find out that things are far from the way we thought they'd be. A strange sense of being lost comes over us and we're not quite sure what to do next. What to fall back on. We see that new problems have succeeded the old ones. Disheartened, throwing up our hands in exasperation, we declare, "It's always something."

Are there completions and milestones to actually look forward to? Are there seasons of life where there's less stress and more enjoyment?

Absolutely. If you sell the family business, sure: you'll no longer be burdened with the daily responsibilities of running it. Great! That's a milestone. Finalize a divorce and you're free of someone who sadly turned out to be a poor fit for your life. But we can't fool ourselves into believing any milestone will find us home free. There *will* always be something. Such is life!

Life doesn't stop presenting us with challenges just because we've checked everything off the to-do list. Postponing joy and happiness by saying, "If this happens, then I'll really start to live," is a sure formula for another three Ds: despair, disappointment, and disillusionment. And what is "really starting to live," anyway?

"Real life" happens in real time: right now. It transpires right here, wherever we are, at any given moment. The real journey is in understanding that most of our joy and happiness in life will not follow a predictable pattern. It's true! Joy can show up anytime. Anywhere. The good stuff is happening while life is progressing, not at some magical future date. There's no point at which we will finally "arrive." Instead, we must learn how to stop and find paradise in every moment.

Remember *The Full Monty*, a hysterically funny movie from the late 1990s where a group of down-and-out steel workers discover a talent for dancing and form a striptease act? There's a great scene in the movie where the men are standing on the unemployment line when a song from their show comes on the loudspeaker. First toes start tapping . . . and then they get into the music and go wild.

That moment came to mind when my friend, Bobbi, told me the story of what had happened to her when she finally gave in to her girl-friends and agreed to go out dancing several months after her divorce had become final. Bobbi didn't want to go, and when she got there, she didn't want to dance. When her friends finally pushed her onto the dance floor, she found her toes moving in time with the music . . . and then her legs. Before long, Bobbi was dancing and shouting and having a blast. Unexpected joy—it's often buried inside us, under the pain, under the sadness, under the grief. But it reemerges, like crocuses peeking through late winter snow, and we feel alive again.

There's no such time or place as "home free." That's our magical thinking selling us a bill of goods. There is only process, a process that we are forever in. Life is a process, and we are a work in progress. The sooner we can accept Real Rule #21, the sooner we can learn how to slow down, take a breath, stop looking for approval, and waiting for things to be perfect. The sooner we can kick up our heels and begin dancing or singing, savoring the moments of sweetness. Including those that show up at the most unexpected times.

Several years ago, I was invited to the funeral of a young African American man named Dante who had been shot and killed in a gang revenge situation. Sadly, the Jenna Druck Center receives calls regularly from families whose kids have been murdered. As I walked from the church with his mother, a young woman carrying a small infant approached us. Earlier I'd seen her sitting with her friends, crying. "Mrs. James," she said to Dante's mother, "You don't know me but I'm your son's girlfriend. And this is your grandson."

Dante's mother had been in the throes of despair since the police had come to her home several days earlier. She thought she had lost everything. Looking down at her grandson, who looked exactly like her son at that age, her grief was tempered by something she thought she'd never experience again. In a moment of despair she had discovered an oasis of unexpected joy.

It's an interesting paradox (by now you are getting used to me saying that) that even though there is no such thing as "home free," at the same time we're *always* "home free." In any given moment, we can be at peace, simply by being present. We *have* arrived! Already!

The peace and deep satisfaction we seek is almost always within reach. If, as the Buddhists say, we can just empty ourselves of all the noise and clutter and suffering created by attachment. Stop the grasping to consume. Stop the incessant searching for status and approval. Stop the relentless mind chatter, and allow in the stillness and silence that flows effortlessly into fullness.

The Gift of Being Present

Sometimes we get so caught up in reaching our goals and feeding our egos that we forget to really be aware of what's happening to us right at this very moment. Maybe we do reach our goal—we've finally made it to the top of the mountain. We clap our hands in victory and say, "I did it! I made it!" And three minutes later, we realize: "How the hell am I going to get down?" Something like that happened to a dear friend of mine. He had been talked into climbing Mt. Kilimanjaro by a younger colleague—and almost died at the top. On the way down the mountain, after his heart had been stabilized, my friend came to a moment of truth. "Despite the fact that I'd almost died, and just wanted a warm bed, my mind almost automatically turned to the future. I began thinking about how I would turn this near-death experience into a great war story for my buddies, and what I could do to top it next year. Rather than be thankful I was alive and grateful to the guys who got me down the mountain, I'd already noticed: 'There's another peak!'"

The nature of human beings is that we are happiest when in pursuit of a worthy goal, not necessarily at the achievement of the goal. The great motivator Earl Nightingale quoted Cervantes as saying, "The road is better than the inn." So when we reach a goal, it's essential to set the next one right away. Perhaps that's what the Founding Fathers meant when they wrote in the Declaration of Independence not about happiness but about the *pursuit* of happiness. If you finish everything on your bucket list, you've got two alternatives—kick the bucket, or write a new list!

And we begin to see that the peaks and valleys can continue unabated for the rest of our lives. Life is a never-ending series of moment-to-moment problems, challenges, and opportunities. There's no way around it. Since things never completely come to rest, it's up to us to cultivate peace of mind in spite of our circumstances. To let the moment be enough—right here, right now. Amidst the incompleteness, the chaos, and the unfinished elements of life. This is home!

Hunter-Gatherers of Meaning

How can our lives have meaning and significance, even without us trying to fill them up every day? Going from being stressed out, adrenalin-addicted, approval-seeking "type E's" (E-verything to E-verybody E-lse) to calmer, more centered "type E's" (E-verything you E-ver wanted to b-E) may not be as difficult as you think. The key is learning to live mindfully. This means slowing down, and freeing our minds from incessant thinking. There is a whole world beyond our thoughts. Achieving this state of mindfulness is unique to each of us. Some of us need a meditation class to learn to "unplug." Others do well with gentle yoga. The there are those who bring themselves to peace through calming music, chanting, and prayer. And still others cultivate an inner stillness by spending more time in nature. Whatever the method, mindfulness simply means learning to live each day, and to approach life, with greater E-ase.

How might you E-ase out of the fast lane, E-ase off the gas pedal, and E-ase up on yourself? Start with the Real Rules in this book—especially those focusing on honesty, self-compassion, bravery, allowing, listening, loving, letting go, and coming to terms with *life's* terms. All of these Real Rules contribute to a life of greater ease, authenticity, joy, connectedness, and simplicity.

How can we live smart in the face of adversity? How, with all the losses and setbacks we may have suffered, can we feel a sense of peace and calm? Surprisingly, it's not by conquering a bigger mountain. But instead, by venturing into the realm of stillness and silence.

How is it possible to begin facing adversity, or to tap into and arrive in this moment by doing nothing? Listening to deeply relaxing music, laying in the soft grass under a cloudless sky, or taking a day or two of silence at a retreat center can all help you unplug and begin to feel your own heartbeat, arrive in this present moment, open your senses, and get centered or feel more grounded. Maybe you've learned to calm and center yourself by cooking a wholesome meal for your family and friends, taking a slow walk on the beach at sunset, or sitting with a crossword puzzle on your favorite chair. Developing the ability to slow your thoughts, self-soothe, be still, and go into silence can be an empowering gift you can give yourself. It's also good preventive medicine for those times when you're being pulled in a hundred directions and you feel like your head is about to fall off. Tempted to jump into the fray and run around with your hair on fire, you find you suddenly have a choice. You can say no, stay grounded, set healthy boundaries, and move through the situation with a new ease. "Effortlessness is best!" I have heard my angel daughter say. But, as I have learned, effortlessness takes practice—especially for those of us who are habitual "doers." But it's a real difference maker. Learning to take a deep breath, step back, and allow things to unfold—rather than exerting and inserting myself into every seductive moment of figuring out and fixing things—has added immeasurable peace to my life. Another great difference maker is the artful practice of beholding.

Beholding 101

We can also learn to arrive in the present moment through the gentle awareness of all that is happening around us. I call this practice "beholding." Behold, here we are speeding through space on a tiny blue planet that is but a speck of dust in the cosmos. And at any given moment, there is more going on than any of us can ever imagine. More than we can possibly fathom.

Getting Real—"Behold Ye"

Note that "behold" is a present-tense action verb, not an esoteric concept. It doesn't mean to regret or reminisce about the past, nor does it mean to project into the future. Beholding takes place right now, in this precious, present moment.

Behold the miracle of a baby being born, a couple getting married, a pink dolphin swimming in the Amazon River, or parents watching their child's first recital or school play. The creation of original art. Laughter and warmth. The thrill of live music and of immeasurable acts of heart-melting kindness. There is boundless, breathless beauty all around us, waiting for us to behold it—to witness it, and lift our hearts in the process.

I recently underwent emergency surgery for, of all things, a spider bite. It became infected and turned into an ugly abscess. The operation left a gaping one-by-three-inch hole in my mid-thigh—about which my daughter, Stefie, helpfully announced, "Dad, that's disgusting." Of course, that didn't stop her from immortalizing it on her new 8-megapixel iPhone.

Rather than stitch me up, the wound was left open to prevent further infection and to allow healing from the inside out ("kind of like grief," I told my girlfriend-turned–wound nurse, Lisette). The pain limited my ability to get around for several weeks but each day as we changed the dressing, I got to behold a small miracle—the healing of my own body. Before my very eyes, new cells of muscle and tissue were forming.

At the same time miracles are happening, we may also behold that there is unspeakable suffering and violence. There is hollowness and hopelessness, misery and despair. There are people who have lost loved ones to war and hunger, mothers who have lost their babies, children who have lost their parents. Marriages and families have been torn apart; lives have been destroyed by natural disasters, catastrophes, toxic waste, and war. There is weeping, and loss, and hearts that have been shattered into a million pieces. There is all of this to somehow fathom and behold.

The ability to be in the moment is to say: "All of this is going on, right now. I am aware of it, and I accept that this is the nature of my human existence. Life being life. I get to be conscious for a moment in time, aware and awake, and to perceive all these things. I get to feel both the suffering and the joy. And, with deep humility, I get to behold all of life unfolding."

Life comes with mysteries. Part of being human means holding the mystery of the unknown. The mystery of all the things we've yet to learn or comprehend—and the things we'll never understand—with great curiosity and humility. We must accept our smallness in the universe, and the fact that we have a very limited idea what it all really means and how it all really works. All we have are signs, clues, and faith. Even if our lifetime is a speck of dust in a flicker of time, we get to stand in this fleeting, eternal moment and be a part of the grand scheme of things. Paradoxically, it is in our humble unknowingness that we become awakened. We become better able to behold and unravel the mystery, and to act honorably all along the way.

Not only do we get to behold the moment; we get to actually help create it. We can have a profound influence on the people around us and even the world by using the full measure of our intelligence, talents, love, vision, and compassion. Our abilities and potential, as so many of my dear friends so brilliantly teach, are far greater than we can possibly comprehend.

Cultivating Ego or Spirit

According to spiritual teacher and author Eckhart Tolle, we have a choice about which part of our nature we cultivate. Our ego—that half-awake part of us that runs around, going through the motions of life, getting us through the day—is strengthened every time we get out of the moment and start projecting into the future. Our spirit—that part of us that aspires to be fully awake—on the other hand, is strengthened when we stay in the moment.

Our ego isn't the enemy, as we have too often been led to believe. In fact we need it to survive. Our ego is a part of our being that's trying to help us establish and maintain our selfhood. Thanks to our egos, we get promoted at work, provide for our families, and go after our dreams. But the ego is too often driven by our insecurities and as such is blind to the realities of the present—not to mention to the world beyond selfhood. And so its utility and usefulness to us is limited when it comes to growing spiritually.

Spiritual awareness and deepening can't be accessed from the ego side. The ego is so busy mapping out our future and crafting step-by-step plans to get us there that it often misses the richness that's right in front of us.

When we favor our ego, it's easy to become self-involved and miss out on what's unfolding around, between, and beyond us. But we can't blame it all on the ego. It's up to us to use the ego as a tool—and to recognize when it's distorting reality and consuming us.

It's only by opening ourselves up to the greater, deeper world beyond ego that we can experience the freedom of living, fully and fearlessly, in the present.

In the moment, we get to pay attention to everything that's already happening. That means the subtle elements of life that are already going on! Right now! Right here! At no time in my life have I been more aware of this than the year following my daughter's death. I was in a state of utter despair and sorrow. There was no place to run, or to hide. No diversions to help me escape from the pain. It was as if I had no skin, no protection, and no filters through which to see and experience the world. I was seeing it as it really was. No pretense. No falseness. No going through the motions. All the noise of day-to-day life had fallen away. My life had dissolved into pain. The past was irrelevant and the future, gone. Standing naked in a season of inescapable sorrow, I began seeing things for what they truly were.

In the years since my own personal holocaust, I've learned that we do not need a tragedy to awaken. There's nothing as wondrous as turning into the pulse of life itself—the heartbeat of the world—and of your soul. You don't have to seek it or create it. It's already right there.

The Saga of Striving and Struggling

The plain truth is that, most of the time, we're only half-awake. The present moment is a gift, but it may not seem like one when we are hurting and struggling. At times of suffering, the "now" can seem more like a royal pain in the butt.

Striving and struggling are a part of life—they can even become addictive, like a drug. Sitting still in the present moment, beholding, and opening our eyes to how things really are can be a tall (and daunting) order; it's much easier to keep a full schedule, a daily routine, and a lifetime agenda where we're forever aspiring to be someone and do something. The irony is that, eventually, the striving and struggling themselves can start to become our MO, and our identity.

"Hey, how ya doin'?"

"Great! Striving and struggling! How 'bout you?"

"Me too. Just reaching my goals! Same ol', same ol'."

And so goes the unspoken transcript of our daily lives. When striving and struggling becomes the theme, the totality, the central organizing principle of our existence, we may be literally missing the opportunity of a lifetime.

If "going through the motions" or "making it through each day" describes you, stop right here!

As scary as it may be, I challenge you to face the moment. To embrace the opportunity of being even more alive and awake.

Buddhism teaches that "waking up" to the present is our only salvation. Only when we are awake can we transcend the frenzied engineering of our lives. There is a deeper truth beyond the mental constructs—a feeling of connection with spirit, with existence, and with something many people call God. No matter what creed you may choose to believe, when you focus on the present you start to see that each of us is a part of something much bigger than just "me."

Transcend the incessant striving of the ego, and you'll find unlimited invitations to peace. Transcend the worldly matters that seem to carry so much weight, and you'll find yourself weightless—awake and alive in a marvelous world of spirit.

Freedom, Unfettered

While "home free" may be a bill of goods, there is great freedom to be had in the present moment. Aligning ourselves to an awakening of spirit is where we find true freedom in this life—not in the bars, restaurants, malls, summer vacations, casinos, or theme parks where we usually go looking for it.

Getting Real—"The Audacity of Freedom"

Freedom lies in being bold. — Robert Frost

One of my consulting clients, Helen, a successful real estate investor, was telling me recently about a risky investment she made.

"For years," she told me, "I'd been telling myself that if this investment worked out, I'd be free—I wouldn't be beholden to anybody. But then I realized that no matter how much money I have in the bank, I'll probably have just as many commitments and obligations as I've always had—if not more."

Many of us have been fooling ourselves when it comes to freedom. We envision lives free of limitations or restraints, imagining ourselves as carefree as the rock stars, sports heroes, and billionaires who are paraded in front of us every day in the media. But in reality, we all have our problems.

Perhaps you consider "home free" to be freedom from certain obligations that are tying you down. Many people feel that freedom is simply the absence of restriction; that we'll be free when we no longer have to do the things we don't want to do. That isn't freedom. Or if it is, it's the fleeting kind.

There's a whole other level of freedom available to us, and that's what I'm talking about here. Freedom to love more freely, to be loved more freely, to be free of guilt, worry, approval, doubt, fear, or pain, and to be freer to express yourself. It's about removing the heaviness and restrictions that hold us back; setting our hearts and minds free. Feeling "enough" within ourselves.

By seeking peace in the moment, we can deepen our understanding of life. And how to best live it. We can learn to balance life's terms with our own. To be courageous. To walk through fire and forests, sail turbulent oceans, unleash our pioneer spirit and sense of wonder. And meet each day with a more profound respect and reverence for living.

This freedom is rarely available to us when we achieve what we thought we wanted. What do we really expect to happen when we write the best-selling book, sell the company for $20 million, or win the lottery? What debt do we expect to get paid off? How much freer do we imagine we'll feel? The reality, while satisfying in its own way, is often far different than what we thought.

There is no "home free." We're already home! And we're already free . . . if we can just learn to slow down a little, remember to breathe, make each day of life more than your "to-do" list, and harvest the subtle riches of the present moment. The "Real Action" exercises at the end of this chapter will show you some great ways to do this. We may feel like aliens at first, living in the now, unplugged from the daily dramas of life. Yet, paradoxically, we are likely to feel more at home than ever. Is it possible that there was never anywhere to go? That we're already there and always have been?

Real Action

RR#21 TAKEAWAYS

True peace, freedom, and contentment aren't lurking around the corner or just beyond the next peak: they're available to us right here, right now. We just have to learn how to live in and relish the present.

EXERCISE #1 Make a list of the old things you've been doing to be "home free."

EXERCISE #2 Now, make a new list of things that will actually allow you to experience freedom and peace.

EXERCISE #3 List five things you could do, or stop doing, to cultivate greater spiritual awakening and peace.

EXERCISE #4 Recall a few moments in your life when beholding something opened your eyes and heart. Write or talk about them to flesh them out.

EXERCISE #5 The following activities can help you cultivate mindfulness and tap into this present moment. Put a check next to one you would be willing to try:

- ❑ Slow my thoughts by learning to breathe and unplug (e.g., do yoga, learn to meditate, or listen to soothing music or relaxation tapes)

- ❑ Get out more into nature where I feel a sense of calm and wonder

- ❑ Sit beside the ocean or in the park and do nothing but relax for at least an hour

Real Rule #22

LET IT BE:
Mastering the Art of Allowing

My first yoga teacher captured the fundamental difference between East and West when she said, "There is no striving or forcing or powering through in this class. It's about *breathing* and *allowing* as you lengthen and strengthen every muscle in your body."

To just "allow" was a novel concept for me. I am used to pushing and striving—powering through those 100 sit-ups; sweating it out running up and down a soccer field. This was a completely different way of approaching fitness. And, as I would come to learn, a completely different way of approaching life.

In the context of yoga, "allowing" means breathing into any area where there's tension, so it gently releases. By simply breathing and releasing, muscles that were tight loosen up and open. When I first began doing yoga, I found myself able to stretch and relax, lengthen and strengthen from within—for the first time. Soon I became flexible and strong.

Getting Real—"The Power of the Breath"

Breathing is essential for two main reasons. First, it is the only means of supplying our bodies and their various organs with the oxygen we need to survive. Second, it is one of the best ways to get rid of waste products and toxins.

Applying the same principle to my life opened a whole new way of being to me. I had become a bit of a control freak, always busy micromanaging situations and running around in circles trying to catch my tail. Thanks to yoga, I learned to take some time every day to just sit down and chill out.

My grandmother Sadie must have understood this. There's an old Yiddish expression she used often—"*Halavai*"—which roughly translates to, "let it be." Sometimes the greatest strides forward aren't made by willfully forcing something. They happen when we breathe, relax, and let it be. I can often hear my angel daughter, Jenna, reminding me, "Effortless is best, Daddy!"

Step in or Step Back?

There are times in life when the best course of action is simply to step back and let things unfold. We talked about the power of surrender in an earlier chapter—how the most powerful thing we can do is step back and get out of our own way. But there are also times when life demands intentionality and effort; when is it appropriate to strive, focus, power through, and take charge. Learning how to discern between the two—or, as singer Kenny Rogers put it—"to know when to hold 'em and know when to fold 'em" is the wise discernment we all seek.

If you're a parent, you've no doubt felt this struggle in very tangible ways. Your relationship with your child is an excellent place to practice striking the right balance. When do you take a hard line, and when do you loosen up on the reins? How do you empower your children to make smart choices? The answer is as unique to you and your child as it is to the specifics of the situation. Opening the lines of communication, listening, building trust, and helping them think through their options is almost always the best approach. This means becoming a facilitator rather than a dictator. It takes practice! Practice may not make perfect, but it does make progress.

We also get opportunities to master this balancing act in business. As we learned in earlier chapters, the most potent strategy for a CEO is not always to storm into the room, put his or her foot down, and say, "Here's the way it's going to be." Sometimes your business will demand that you play hardball, but it can't be that way all the time. Historically speaking, dictatorships haven't proven very effective. One of the most rewarding parts of my work is coaching leaders to facilitate exceptional meetings, empower their teams, make great decisions, and watch their employees flourish.

There are tremendous benefits to CEO's and parents—all of us for that matter—in knowing when it's time to hold and when it's time to fold. When to just relax and allow. Life requires many gears; we need to be able to downshift at will. These are the times when we let go and allow things to unfold with patience and ease. As my yoga teacher used to say, "If you're the kind of person who tends to hold back, push in a little. If, on the other hand, you tend to push too hard, ease up a bit."

Sometimes easing up, itself, is an agent of change in the world. People see how relaxed we are and they begin to relax. The opposite is also true: when people see how tense we are, they tense up, too. Often it's only when we slow down and ease up that we achieve the very change we were fighting so hard for in the first place.

Getting Real—"Time to Hold" vs. "Time to Fold"

There are times when it's important to stick to your guns and hold fast to your beliefs. There are other times when it's important to breathe, relax, and allow—to let go and discover the change that is already unfolding.

Each of us has to create our own sense of balance and mastery, often through trial and error. If we're fortunate, along the way we enjoy the guidance of great friends, parents, teachers, and coaches and our own wise-beyond-their-years children. As the Dalai Lama said, "Cultivating an attitude of compassion and developing wisdom are slow processes . . . You will need to practice these techniques day by day, year by year. As you transform your mind, you will transform your surroundings. Others will see the benefits of your practice of tolerance and love, and will work at bringing these practices into their own lives."

Taking a Step Back and Settling Down

There's no better (or more challenging) place to practice Real Rule #22 than in our families. I still catch myself burning to say something— to air my feelings, defend my position, and let it be known where I stand with my family. And yet, there are times when the best thing to do is to say nothing at all—but simply to listen. (I have scar tissue on the tip of my tongue from all the times I have had to bite it.)

This is especially true after a period of turmoil. When we've just experienced an ordeal, our nervous systems and brains need a period in which they can settle. Everything needs time to cure—whether it's pottery, asphalt, tempers, or hearts.

A period of settlement is often the actual factor in a breakthrough, because it's only after that settlement that we're ready to have the conversation or take the action that will move us forward. We have to ground and reconfigure things inside of us before we can change the world. This does not happen instantaneously or automatically. We need to consciously step back and come up for air. Subtle changes are often made in stillness and silence where we can calmly reflect about and choose best-case scenarios.

And, of course, the opposite can also be true. Sometimes we need to just speak up. Many of us were brought up in families where there were "elephants" (i.e., undeclared, unspoken conflicts, tensions, resentments, and grudges)—and more—sitting smack in the middle of the room. These things were never named or acknowledged or discussed, yet they helped shape our family relationships, personalities, and styles of communication. They also affected our ability to be intimate, forthright, open, and honest, both with ourselves and others.

There are also times when we know the elephant is there, but the best thing to do is to breathe and say nothing. It's the letter we write to an ex but never send. The criticism we are wise to hold back from an already defensive child. It's the thoughts we have but never need to speak, the hurtful thing we know we could say to our boss but choose not to. It's the defensive reaction we contain during a fight, because we know what needed to be said is already in the air. It's understanding that a period of gestation, restraint, and healing is often required before a positive outcome is possible.

This can be especially difficult when we're feeling extremely angry, frustrated, scared, or sad. But at some point, words and emotions can lose their value. And can actually do harm. There's no sense, as the saying goes, in beating a dead horse! We just have to trust that, at times, most everything has already been said. The most we can do is to take a deep breath, clear our thoughts, and let things unfold of their own accord.

Real Action

RR#22 TAKEAWAYS

Are you prone to "powering through"? If so, you're definitely not alone—we live in a world obsessed with speed, efficiency, and quick results. We want to power through our days as effectively and quickly as possible, blowing past any obstacles in our way. But what would it look like to simply allow once in a while?

EXERCISE #1 Try out these everyday tips as a way to "let it be":

- Next time you're in a heated discussion, resist the urge to have the last word.

- Recognize that you don't have to say every last thing on your mind in every situation. Learn to selectively bite your tongue.

- Next time you're frustrated with someone, make a conscious choice to step back and view them with compassion. You'll be amazed at how this can shift your perceptions and the entire tone of the conversation.

EXERCISE #2 Rate yourself on a scale from 1 to 10 in the "knows when to hold" vs. "knows when to fold" department, with 10 being the best score.

EXERCISE #3 List one thing you could do to raise your score, such as "be more patient" or "get my ego out of the way," and where you might try it out the next chance you get.

Real Rule #23

YOUR LIFE IS YOUR BIRTHRIGHT:
Live It As Though

Each of us goes through periods of reflection and insight, searching and contemplation. Whether we've experienced an epiphany, are healing after a great loss, or are trying to prevent one, we gain much strength, clarity, and understanding from listening to our own hearts and keeping an open mind. After we've read an inspiring book, listened to a great speaker, or attended a great seminar, we are inspired to ask ourselves, "What next? What can I do to make my life better? What are the next steps?"

At the end of every coaching session or consultation, I have my clients draw up an action plan. They begin with, "Because I'm smart, I will . . ." In other words, it's time to make a decision and take action. What will you actually do now with all that you have learned in these pages, including your own notes to yourself?

Getting Real—"An Action Plan"

An action plan isn't meant to set up unattainable ideals or give you a laundry list of goals you'll beat yourself up for never attaining. On the contrary: it should give you hope and inspiration—a feasible, actionable plan for going after the things you want most in life.

My hope is that, as you've read through the Real Rules and gained some greater awareness about how your life really is, you've been inspired to action. That the thoughts and ideas in these pages have ignited new and old inspirations for you—things to try, reminders to act, truths to embrace, options to exercise, and guidelines to live by. And that you have taken the opportunity to activate your mind and heart by doing the suggested exercises at the end of every chapter.

Hopefully, one or more of these rules has sparked a desire within you, uncovering a seed for change. Maybe it's a phone call you could make or an apology that's long overdue. It could be a relationship you want to start or work on, or one you're finally ready to leave. It might be a simple awareness about the need to be kinder toward yourself. To free yourself and become more of a risk taker. Or, at the other end of the spectrum, perhaps you've seen the need to become more discerning. Whatever you've discovered, these are the gifts that the Real Rules are designed to bring to fruition.

Perhaps there was also a Real Rule, or something you read, that didn't resonate with what you know to be true—something that doesn't jibe with what you've felt. Trust your own experience. These rules are but one man's truth. I encourage you to go to the feedback section of www.kendruck.com and add your suggestions for how I might make the rule truer and more relevant. Or add another Real Rule, all your own. My readers have always been some of my greatest teachers.

You have the ability and the power to set the terms you want in this life; to decide what you want from yourself and your relationships and to make changes that will get you there. It is your birthright. And that's the Real Rule for this final chapter.

Yes, life has its own terms. Life will have its say, and we don't get to play God—as several of the Real Rules remind us. But that should not stop you from fiercely pursuing, understanding, and creating the life you want. You have every right to set your own terms. Bold or simple. And to honor them by the way you live each day.

Growing Our Souls

The best place for setting our terms and growing our souls is in relationships—relationships with each other, with the world we live in, and with ourselves. "God is the love that occurs between us and others," my dear and wise friend Terry teaches. Relationships present us with an ongoing test for authenticity and integrity, as well as for engaging fully with life. You might say they are the growing fields of life.

Many of us have become pleasers and accommodators. We become so malleable in the spirit of avoiding conflict, making peace, and connecting with others, we forget that we're allowed to live authentically and set our own terms. In fact, not only are we "allowed" to; we must! Sooner or later, we have to learn to say, "Here are the terms under which life works best for me. And here are the terms under which it doesn't." This term-setting doesn't come from a position of rigid arrogance or narcissism, but from being centered in your own truth.

Setting healthier boundaries is required for spiritual growth and successful relationships. If you can clearly and courageously set your terms, it means you've come to know yourself well enough to know what works and doesn't work for you. What you like and what you don't like. The times you feel respected and the times you don't. When you feel someone's support and when you don't. Not only are you allowed to know your terms; it's your birthright to ask for them, and to fiercely negotiate your relationships with those terms in mind. That's authenticity, and with it comes real growth.

The coaching I do with couples is invariably about setting healthy boundaries. Open, respectful communication on core issues like time management, sex, co-parenting, and keeping agreements about finances are a hundred times more likely to draw them closer. We end up discovering, rather than losing, more of ourselves in our relationship.

Getting Real—"Relationships as Soul Food"

Personal and spiritual growth is best attained in our relationships with other people; you can't get that anywhere else. The primary benefit of our relationships is to grow our souls by learning to love.

There's no more humbling experience than being in a real, vulnerable, human relationship. And, incidentally, there's probably nothing we're less prepared to do in this life. What template do we have for being in relationships? Some of us were fortunate enough to grow up in homes and communities where there were constructive ways of dealing with love, communication, support, and conflict; others of us weren't so lucky. Even those of us who did grow up with healthy role models may still struggle to connect intimately and authentically with other human beings.

Why? Probably because there's no handbook for love. Relationships are where all of our blind spots, distortions, insecurities, unmet needs, and deepest desires for love are likely to emerge. Our greatest hopes and deepest fears show up in our relationships—in fact they're eventually brought directly into the limelight. Stay in a relationship long enough and all of the frontline defenses that you learned growing up will at some point be rendered useless, if not harmful.

As most of us have learned from hard-earned experience, relationships force us to learn much healthier, better defenses. To grow new skin and discover more selfless, unconditional ways of loving. We learn how to set healthy boundaries so we don't lose ourselves in someone else. How to negotiate, cooperate, communicate, and commit. It's everything we tried to learn in kindergarten, only this time around, the stakes are much higher. Our relationships call us to a higher level of intimacy, authenticity, creativity, and connectedness—one we would likely have never reached on our own. Perhaps, most of all, we learn to love and be loved.

Over coffee one afternoon, Del, a neighbor of mine whose wife was diagnosed with cancer, tearfully confessed, "Did it really take one of us getting sick to realize how much we love each other, Ken? It's like we've been asleep all these years. Now, we can't wait until the end of each day because that's when we get to hold each other. I cannot imagine my life without her."

One of the great accomplishments of a lifetime is to be able to feel a sense of oneness with another human being—to learn that level of joy and selfless giving. To access a kind of loving where we don't lose ourselves; rather, we realize the greater expression of ourselves in our ability to truly be intimate. To do this, we must be connected to our own soul, that of another person, and the wondrous totality of the world around us.

Someday, we will relinquish our lives. On that day, we will let go of our own individual identity and become a part of what the Buddhists call "the great everything." It's where we came from, and it's where we will return. Better to let go, a little at a time, while we are still alive. To look at life with great humility.

There are a lot of lingering myths about why we're here. We often act as if our purpose is to make a lot of money, become successful, or achieve a certain status for ourselves and our families. We may act as if we're on earth for material success and status, but our hearts yearn at the core for connection—connection to our true selves, to the people we love, to our fellow earthlings, to nature and to that which is greater than us. The more we focus on strengthening those connections, the greater life will reward us with peace.

My connections to people, and to life itself, have deepened over the years. I've worked hard to live as much of my life as possible on my terms and learned to humbly surrender when life is setting its own.

Early one morning, 15 years ago, I drove my daughter, Jenna, to the airport where she was flying to meet her Semester At Sea study abroad program. Jenna would be living on a ship and traveling around the world for the next several months. As we walked to the gate, I told her she was about to go on "the adventure of a lifetime."

"Daddy, I'm a little scared," she confessed. "I've never been this far away from my family for this long."

I was one of the few people she would say that to; to the world she was a pillar of strength. I replied, "I'm scared too, sweetie, but this trip is going to be a launching pad for the rest of your life. I can't wait for you to come home and tell us all about the places you've been and people you've met." Jenna and I tearfully hugged and kissed each other good-bye. Minutes later, I watched her flight disappear into the morning sky. I never saw my daughter again.

Fast forward ten years. I am at the airport with my daughter Stefie, who is going to tour the great cities of Italy. Stef has struggled horribly since her sister's death and this trip represented a triumph of courage. It's everything in my power to hold back tears, knowing the assurances I'd given her sister were empty promises. My heart is tied in knots. Stefie may be going on the trip of her lifetime, but I cannot say so. I can't even say she is going to come home. All I can do is hope, pray, and manage to say, "Have a great time, sweetheart, and please come home safe. I love you so much."

Stefie knew what I was thinking. She gave me a reassuring smile, hugged me extra tight and reassured me, "Everything's going to be all right, Daddy. I love you." Stefie's plane soon disappeared into the morning sky and I walked slowly to my car. Closing the car door, the tears came. I'd sent another precious daughter out into the world. Like Jenna, she would be at the mercy of forces beyond my understanding. Fate? Luck? Gravity? Karma? I really didn't care. All I wanted was my daughter back.

Ten days and three hours later, Stefie's flight landed safely back in San Diego. We cried tears of joy and talked for hours about her many adventures in Italy. That night, as I got into bed and turned on the evening news, I could breathe a sigh of relief. I watched as the wives, husbands, parents, and children of men and women leaving for Iraq said good-bye to their beloved husbands, sons, and daughters. My heart ached for them, knowing some of them would not come home. The families of those brave men and women they were sending into the world were at the mercy of life's terms. And they would not be breathing for quite some time.

Act Now!

So much wisdom has been given to us through everyday life. Music, books, movies, plays, sermons, speeches, teachings, revelations, the natural world, and deeply inspiring *encounters* touch us at the core and bless us with a wealth of resources. The way we honor everything we've been given is to take at least one thing that's touched us, one thing that's real, and to act on it.

As you prepare to finish this book, ask yourself, "If there's one thing I would take from *The Real Rules of Life,* one way I could turn what I have read into action, it would be . . ." Look back through your notes and the pages you marked because they meant something special to you. Then, fill in the blank however you choose.

It could be one simple act, or it could be a great act on the behalf of many people. It could be an expression of gratitude or kindness. It could be a gift to the world or a gift to yourself—a rededication to your mission in life.

Doing this takes courage, diligence, and strength of heart. Living with integrity, aligning ourselves with the highest good, facing the tough times and the aloneness and the unknowingness and the sorrow—all the things we've talked about in this book. Learning to love ourselves from compassion and not from criticism. Learning to be patient, kind, and encouraging with ourselves and others.

It isn't always easy. It's not supposed to be. But it is so worth it, this work we do on ourselves to become the better version of us.

The time has come for you to stop reading and move on. Don't just think about the Real Rules—though I hope they've given you much to ponder. Don't just talk about them—though I hope you tell people what you've learned. No, now is the time to act. Now is the time to *live.*

May you receive all the many blessings, rich and resounding, of this crazy adventure called life. And may we meet again on the path.

Ken Druck
October 2011

✧ ✧ ✧

Real Action

The Real Rules of Life are tools for creating real love, hope, joy, health, and forward movement in your life. Are you ready to put them to use?

EXERCISE #1 Draw up an action plan for what you want from your life. Be sure to include:

- Your vision and dreams

- Your deepest desires

- Your greatest hopes

- Your curiosities and yet-to-be-taken adventures

- The things that bring you the greatest joy

EXERCISE #2 Complete the statement, "Because I'm smart, I will . . ." Feel free to draw liberally from your notes and the material you've read on these pages.

I'd love to continue to help you on your journey. I invite you to contact me through my website: **www.kendruck.com** or at **Druck Enterprises Inc., P.O. Box. 1117, Del Mar, California, 92014.** Remember, the journey can be long and daunting, but it's worth every beautiful, heartbreaking, glorious moment.

✧ ✧ ✧

ABOUT THE AUTHOR

Ken Druck, Ph.D., is one of the nation's pioneers in personal transformation, breaking fresh ground in male psychology, executive coaching, organizational consulting, parent effectiveness, healing after loss, and, most recently, the art of turning adversity into opportunity. Druck Enterprises, Inc. (DEI) is a leading coaching, consulting, and team-building firm with a broad base of clients including Microsoft, Pfizer, IBM, *U-T San Diego,* and the YMCA.

Since founding The Jenna Druck Center in 1996, "Dr. Ken" has become a lifeline for thousands of families who have suffered a loss. He is often called upon to assist in healing after tragic events such as 9/11, the shootings at Columbine High School, and Hurricane Katrina.

Ken is the author of *The Secrets Men Keep: Breaking the Silence Barrier, Healing Your Life After the Loss of a Loved One,* and *How to Talk to Your Kids About School Violence.* He has also authored chapters in a variety of books including *Chicken Soup for the Grieving Soul.*

In recent years, Ken has been the recipient of the Visionary Leadership, Distinguished Contribution to Psychology, and Family Advocate awards. He is a standing member of the Transformational Leadership Council (www.transformationalleadershipcouncil.com) and regular contributor to several global leadership initiatives. He also recently co-founded and serves on the nation's first Community Editorial Board at *U-T San Diego,* where he is a frequent (and outspoken) editorial contributor.

Website: **www.kendruck.com**

WANT TO GO DEEPER?

If *The Real Rules of Life* spoke to you, and you'd like to go deeper,
please visit Ken Druck's official website
www.RealRulesofLife.com
to bring Dr. Druck's work into your life, beginning with a **Free Download** of
The Real Rules Workbook on Self-Coaching and complimentary four-week
audio coaching program to get you on track.

To hire Ken as an executive coach, consultant, or facilitator; have him as a speaker; or register to attend one of his workshops, please go to **www.KenDruck.com** or contact his offices directly at (858) 86DRUCK. You can also sign up to receive special announcements, blogs, and exclusive tools for personal and professional development at either location.

Coaching: As one of the pioneers of executive coaching, Ken Druck has worked extensively over the past three decades with individuals, families, couples, and CEO's, turning their greatest challenges into opportunities for personal, interpersonal, professional, and spiritual growth.

Consulting: Take your organization to the next level with Dr. Ken Druck as your consultant. Working with executives and their management teams, boards, and family business and communities, Ken has consistently turned even the most challenging situations into opportunities for peak effectiveness and team building with organizations of every type and size.

Speaking: Voted "Best of YPO" and having keynoted for audiences of more than 15,000 people, Dr. Ken Druck is a powerful and refreshingly original platform speaker who speaks from firsthand knowledge and experience—and always from his heart. Each of his talks is guaranteed to be a life-changing, deeply inspiring experience for any audience.

Workshops: With master facilitator and workshop leader, Ken Druck, you are guaranteed to learn, grow, heal, and connect on an entirely new level. Ken's workshops are offered throughout the year and worldwide.

THE JENNA DRUCK CENTER

The Jenna Druck Center is a 501(c)(3) nonprofit foundation started by Ken Druck in 1996 to honor the life and spirit of his daughter.

The Center's **Families Helping Families** (FHF) Program provides support and education to families, schools, organizations, and communities who have suffered the loss of a loved one. Their **Spirit of Leadership** Program provides year-round leadership conferences, workshops, and programs to empower and educate young women in middle and high school.

For information, or to make a tax-deductible donation, please contact **The Jenna Druck Center** online at www.jennadruckcenter.org, call (619) 294-8000, e-mail info@jennadruck.org, or write to 2820 Roosevelt Rd., Suite 200, San Diego, CA. 92106.

Hay House Titles of Related Interest

YOU CAN HEAL YOUR LIFE, *the movie*, starring Louise L. Hay & Friends
(available as a 1-DVD program and an expanded 2-DVD set)
Watch the trailer at: **www.LouiseHayMovie.com**

THE SHIFT, *the movie*,
starring Dr. Wayne W. Dyer
(available as a 1-DVD program and an expanded 2-DVD set)
Watch the trailer at: **www.DyerMovie.com**

✦ ✦ ✦

EXCUSES BEGONE!: *How to Change Lifelong, Self-Defeating
Thinking Habits*, by Dr. Wayne W. Dyer

INSIDE-OUT HEALING: *Transforming Your Life Through the
Power of Presence*, by Richard Moss

IT'S NOT THE END OF THE WORLD: *Developing Resilience
in Times of Change*, by Joan Borysenko, Ph.D.

SHIFT HAPPENS!: *How to Live an Inspired Life . . . Starting Right Now!*,
by Robert Holden, Ph.D.

✦ ✦ ✦

All of the above are available at your local bookstore,
or may be ordered by contacting Hay House (see next page).

✦ ✦ ✦

We hope you enjoyed this Hay House book. If you'd like to receive our online catalog featuring additional information on Hay House books and products, or if you'd like to find out more about the Hay Foundation, please contact:

Hay House, Inc., P.O. Box 5100, Carlsbad, CA 92018-5100
(760) 431-7695 or (800) 654-5126
(760) 431-6948 (fax) or (800) 650-5115 (fax)
www.hayhouse.com® • **www.hayfoundation.org**

Published and distributed in Australia by: Hay House Australia Pty. Ltd., 18/36 Ralph St., Alexandria NSW 2015 • *Phone:* 612-9669-4299 • *Fax:* 612-9669-4144 www.hayhouse.com.au

Published and distributed in the United Kingdom by: Hay House UK, Ltd., 292B Kensal Rd., London W10 5BE • *Phone:* 44-20-8962-1230 • *Fax:* 44-20-8962-1239 www.hayhouse.co.uk

Published and distributed in the Republic of South Africa by: Hay House SA (Pty), Ltd., P.O. Box 990, Witkoppen 2068 • *Phone/Fax:* 27-11-467-8904 • www.hayhouse.co.za

Published in India by: Hay House Publishers India, Muskaan Complex, Plot No. 3, B-2, Vasant Kunj, New Delhi 110 070 • *Phone:* 91-11-4176-1620 • *Fax:* 91-11-4176-1630 www.hayhouse.co.in

Distributed in Canada by: Raincoast, 9050 Shaughnessy St., Vancouver, B.C. V6P 6E5 *Phone:* (604) 323-7100 • *Fax:* (604) 323-2600 • www.raincoast.com

Take Your Soul on a Vacation

Visit **www.HealYourLife.com®** to regroup, recharge, and reconnect with your own magnificence. Featuring blogs, mind-body-spirit news, and life-changing wisdom from Louise Hay and friends.

Visit **www.HealYourLife.com** today!